THE
HOME
EDIT

THE HOME EDIT

CONQUERING *the* CLUTTER *with* STYLE

CLEA SHEARER & JOANNA TEPLIN

MITCHELL BEAZLEY

CONTENTS

INTRODUCTION:
If We Can Do It, You Can Do It — 8

THE *Edit*
24

THE *Assembly*
52

THE *Upkeep*
242

HOW TO STAY INSPIRED — 247

THANKS — 251

INDEX — 253

If We Can Do It,
YOU CAN
DO IT

If you're feeling even a little bit overwhelmed at the thought of organizing your home, you should immediately breathe a sigh of relief. Because truthfully, we at The Home Edit are barely capable of simple tasks like ironing or cooking rice (Do you leave it covered? Uncovered? Do you need to stir? *Why is it so complicated??*). But what we are good at is walking into a room, seeing past the mess, and coming up with a methodical plan of attack. So if we can somehow create sense out of chaos, we bet you can, too.

When we first launched The Home Edit (or THE, as we are often called), we had a very clear objective: Transform the way people think about organization. Now . . . we understand we're not performing brain surgery or curing cancer. BUT we've seen firsthand how powerful it c an be to create a clutter-free space and make it exceptionally functional— whether it's the kids being able to help themselves to a cereal station in the pantry (we'll do anything to get thirty more minutes of sleep) or finally being able to see your clothes in the closet after clearing away twenty years' worth of nostalgia (no, your daughter will not want that shirt one day).

We weren't satisfied with being just another couple of organizers who could sort things into bins and use a label maker. We wanted our spaces to function and *look beautiful.* So we figured out a unique system that adds a layer of visual aesthetic alongside the practical one—much in the same way a designer approaches a space.

We didn't do this because it looked amazing on Instagram or because we really (really) like when things are organized in rainbow order—we did it because we believe that organizing spaces shouldn't just be about putting things in their place. Nor should it just be about the way the room looks. We wanted to showcase the magical sweet spot that exists where function meets form—when spaces are efficient, user-friendly, and aesthetically pleasing all at once. It not only makes sections of your home more enjoyable to look at, but we've also found that sprinkling this extra layer of pixie dust inspires people to *maintain their organized spaces.* Which is the whole point! If, as our client, you're not able to maintain the systems we put in place, then we didn't do our jobs effectively.

If we were to go back to your home a year later, we'd want to see that The Home Edit is still working for you. Literally the first thing we do when revisiting a client's home is to check to see if that vanity drawer or linen closet looks like we organized it last week; if so, we give ourselves a shiny gold star. And guess what? We have a sticker chart FULL of gold stars because the systems we create really *do* work. (Obviously we keep track of these things because we love accomplishments almost as much as we love sticker charts.)

It wasn't long before we started to feel like something bigger was happening. Clients all over the country, including Gwyneth Paltrow, Molly Sims, Rachel Zoe, Tiffani Thiessen, and Mindy Kaling, were requesting our services. And then we started to see our work splashed across *Domino, Architectural Digest,* the *Today* show, and even the Target website (which was probably the most exciting thing to ever happen to us—no offense to our children). The more exposure we received, the more people asked us, "How on earth can I do that in *my* home? Surely whipping my house into perfect Gwyneth-worthy synchronization is expensive, time-consuming, and requires a team of people." Honestly, that's not true. We're not gonna lie, organizing can be hard—it requires work, time, and thoughtfulness, and it can be more emotional than people expect. But if you have a system in place and rules to follow—and you don't bite off more than you can chew—you can get there. And you can trust us on this, because if we can do it, pretty much anyone can do it! (See "Are You a Good Candidate for Organization?," page 19.)

THE *Backstory*

Before we were organizers, we were just regular people doing average things. Maybe even mediocre people doing less than average things. And we didn't start out as organizers. We didn't even start out wanting to create this company together in the first place. In fact, WE'D NEVER EVEN MET BEFORE. It's true. So before we continue with all the organization stuff that you actually bought this book for, let us first tell you a little bit about us . . . Actually, we're going to let our friend Leah tell you about how we met, since she introduced us.

LEAH'S HOT TAKE *on How We Met*

Clea first moved to Nashville in May 2015. Upon arriving, she thought, *Okay, I'm a thirty-three-year-old woman in a brand-new city and know zero people. We moved our family here for my husband's career, but NOW WHAT?!* Cue the panic attack. Before the move, Clea had considered starting an organizing company, but that made a lot more sense back in LA where she had an existing network (of significantly more than zero people). So even though it made no sense whatsoever, she decided "things that make sense" had never played a role in her decision-making, and she was going to start an organizing business regardless of where she lived.

Right after she moved to Nashville, Clea and I became Instagram friends (how else do adults become friends nowadays?), and we quickly moved our online relationship to a real-life breakfast date. We talked about kids, our husbands, being Jewish transplants in Nashville (there are like eleven of us), and owning a small business. She said she was considering starting a full-service home organization company, and I was like, "WHOA, WAIT. I have another friend named Joanna—also Jewish, also has two kids, also has a husband in the music industry, also just moved to Nashville—and she wants to start an organizing company here, too!" So I'm thinking, *This is so great! They are going to love each other!*

Meanwhile, I call Joanna and tell her about her new destiny and she was like, *"No way, no how, no thank you."* More specifically, she said, "I just don't want a business partner. I'm fine going to lunch with her and MAYBE even having a new friend, but I've never had a partner before and it just won't work." *Well, that went well,* I thought. At least they were going to *lunch*. I wasn't holding my breath for anything else. And I certainly didn't expect their lunch to turn into four hours discussing ideas for worldwide organizing domination. And the rest is history! YOU ARE WELCOME.

xo, LEAH

It was obvious from the minute we met that we would be starting a business together. And later that night, after our four-hour lunch, while we were half-giving our kids baths, we were also half-figuring out the future of our business via text. We came up with our name, The Home Edit, secured the domain name and our social handles, and even started filing the LLC paperwork. Organizers are nothing if not efficient, right? Of course, years later we're both like, *I can't believe I went into business with someone I knew for only a few hours and didn't do a background check or even a thorough Google search.* It's also hilarious because we were introduced by a mutual "friend" . . . but that person was an online friend from Instagram. Not the most advisable course of action, but we don't always take the advisable course. After all, we had both moved to a city we had never even set foot in, where none of our friends or family lived—so we figured we might as well continue down the path of following our gut instinct.

Sure, it's just about the craziest thing we've ever done, but it worked out. Chalk it up to "Jewish Stuff + Magic Tricks" (see page 50). We both went with our intuition, which, as it turned out, is what makes us so well suited for each other. We may be *completely* different people with varying champagne and candy needs, but we also have plenty of similarities! We both have the ability to tap in to our instincts and just *do*. We don't mess around with analyzing things until we're blue in the face. We just go for it and make it happen, whether it's building a business from scratch, making sense of other people's messes, or coming up with solutions for any obstacles we encounter. Sometimes we find ourselves in a work-induced shopping spiral because of it (apologies to our husbands), but that's another story for another time.

Our differences also work really well together when it comes to organizing spaces. Clea worked in the fashion industry and went to art school, and her approach to organization typically comes from an aesthetic standpoint. Joanna, on the other hand, comes from a more traditional organizing background, which has function as the star of the show. We each balance the other in terms of style and utility—especially because we both firmly believe in how important being organized is for a home to operate effectively and efficiently, and how crucial it is for peace of mind.

YOU KNOW YOU ARE AN OBSESSIVE ORGANIZER WHEN . . .

1. You mentally (and sometimes actually) start rearranging store displays.

2. You always wonder why Starbucks doesn't line up their sweeteners in rainbow order because it feels like SUCH a missed opportunity.

3. You consider cleaning up to be your main source of cardio.

4. Your friends think it's funny to rearrange things in your house to see if you notice (YES, WE ALWAYS NOTICE, PLEASE STOP).

5. You label anything that isn't moving.

We know people think we're a little nuts. I mean, who on earth sets out to be an organizer? You'd have to be an insane person to want to volunteer to deal with people's pasta back stock and piles of sweaters every day. So when people ask us why we do what we do, we tell them it's because we're not good at anything else. This is literally the only thing we're good at. We're really just talented in this one focused area (thank goodness we found something)! And in case you can't tell, we're really, really passionate about it, too. Because it's not just our job; it's truly the inner workings of our brains on display. We get excited when we walk into a house and there are messy drawers everywhere. We love peeling back the layers to help get to the root of what makes a space so frustrating for someone—and what the best solutions will be. And pretty soon . . . *you* will know what solutions will work in those messy drawers (so get ready for some nerdy excitement of your own!).

It's not because we're gold-star-collecting egomaniacs (although we do love those gold stars). It's because we are constantly asked questions about organizing and how people can go about doing it themselves, and we want to finally answer as many of them as we can. We want to give *you* the tools to bring peacefulness and order to your home. We want to help you finally wrap your head around not just what needs to go where, but *why*. And ultimately, just like with our clients, we want you to be happy with the end result. We want you to feel good about your house and your own organizing abilities! So often we hear "I'm just not that kind of person." But you *totally* can be. And not only are we going to get you there, but we're going to help you feel confident that your organizational systems will work for the long run.

CHECK IT OUT

There is nothing more satisfying than an organized fridge (admittedly biased), so we included a set of THE fridge labels at the back of the book to get you started!

Are You a Good Candidate for ORGANIZATION?

We've said it before—you don't have to be a professional organizer to be good at putting things in their place. All you need is a basic understanding of the process, a healthy dose of inner honesty, and a host of strategies, tools, tips, and tricks to help you figure out how to best organize your space. Still not convinced that you can do as we do? Ask yourself these questions:

1. Is there a tiny piece of my brain that feels calmer when things have a "place"?

2. Is there something in my mind that flicks on when I see something really organized?

3. Do I believe organizing my belongings will make my life easier?

   If you said yes to any of those questions, then you have what it takes to tackle any project in this book. Whether you'll be good at it is irrelevant—we're going to help you get good at it. What's most important is that you *want* to do it.

THE *Promise*

Assuming you're not as impatient as we are and haven't already flipped ahead to learn how to transform your junk drawer (okay, see page 193), let's talk about why organizing is so important. Believe us when we say that if it were just about staging spaces for gorgeous pictures, we would have been out of business a long time ago. Not only because spaces that are pretty for pretty's sake are not designed to last that way, but also because organizing a space is a lot more meaningful than just aesthetics. Figuring out why you feel compelled to bring order to your home is just about as important as knowing how to do it. Without that piece, it's much harder to motivate yourself to clean out those shelves and drawers, and it's even more difficult to keep them that way in the months that follow. So even though we know you're raring to go, take a minute to appreciate the most common ways organization can benefit you and your family, and keep them in the back of your mind as you choose which space to tackle first.

1. **It's a time-saver.** Pretty simple math here—if you know where something's stored, it's quicker to find and easier to put away.

2. **It's a money-saver.** Aside from the initial investment in infrastructure (drawer dividers, bins, baskets, hooks, etc.), being able to actually see your things means not overbuying toilet paper/cereal/T-shirts/packing tape because you can't find what you have or you didn't know you already had it. And allotting a specific amount of space to certain items means you won't buy more until there's room for more.

3. **It's a sanity-saver.** As moms and wives ourselves, we're often the household gatekeepers—but each home has its own go-to person who knows where everything lives. Whether it's snacks, toothpaste, or hair ties, it's helpful when everything has a place, and those places are easily accessible. Then *everyone* can learn where things live, how to help themselves, and, best of all, how to put things away. This is one of the reasons we love organizing playroom spaces. It not only looks great and encourages creativity, but it also provides a visual system for kids so they can help with the cleanup.

4. **It provides closure.** It's no secret that we assign emotional significance to our belongings, and that attachment is very powerful. The best way to feel a sense of release or closure is by appropriately handling the things that are weighing you down (whether or not you realize that they are). Maybe closure comes from donating baby clothes when you know in your heart you're not going to have another one, or even packing up jeans that you want to be able to fit in one day. We do not take these projects lightly since they require us to tread delicately. People often resist taking these projects on themselves because of the inherent emotional land mines that exist; one of our clients, for example, put off organizing her photo collection because she had recently lost her mother. No one wants to deal with those feelings, but we also know that by working the steps and clearing the space (physically and emotionally), you will find healthy and satisfying relief.

5. **It's calming.** One of the things we love most about having organized homes, and one of the things we often hear from our clients, is how calm they feel when everything's put away. When you're in a space where clutter is minimized and systems prevail, you feel more grounded, like you can take a breath. There aren't black-hole cabinets or closets tugging at the back of your mind. Everything feels settled. Most of our clients tell us that after we've made over their spaces, they feel less stress. If all that stands between you and tranquillity is a paint pen and some acrylic bins, we're happy to oblige!

EVEN ORGANIZERS *Need Help Organizing*

This book is arranged the way it is for a reason—to help you achieve the best results without getting completely overwhelmed; to help your space reach its maximum potential; and to help you maintain that space and its gorgeous organization for the long term. The process we'll walk you through here is no different from how we'd be working together if you hired us to come to your home in person. So no matter how organized you consider yourself, we urge you to follow the plan— because it works!

And because of this fact: Even organizers need guidance. That's right—even the most methodical, orderly, type A people benefit from having an unbiased, objective, nonemotional party helping them down the path.

Believe it or not, we know firsthand how difficult it can be to tackle a big, scary project . . . like writing a book, for instance. We just couldn't figure out where to start, and organizing your home can conjure up similar emotions. So we did what any mature adults would do and asked for a little help to get on the right track. And what do you know— organizing a book is no different from organizing a space: You have to take inventory of everything you want in there, clean out what you don't, sort items by type, identify how to make those items as accessible as possible, and then make the whole thing look nice. But even though we know that process so well it's imprinted in our DNA, we had a hard time following the steps without a guide because this was foreign territory (see page 9). Hopefully, as you start your organizing adventures, this book can act as *your* guide. Because we are *all* in the "OMG PLEASE HELP ME" club and not ashamed one bit!

the edit

That first night after our fateful lunch, when we were texting instead of making sure our children were somewhat bathed, we racked our brains to come up with the perfect name for our business. We tried several combinations, but once we landed on "The Home Edit," there was no turning back. We wanted our name to articulate the core of our organizing philosophy: Edit everything. Or, more specifically, always start the organizing process by paring down your items to the ones that are most used, most loved, and most important. It's an idea that's summed up by our logo, a clean, simple monogram nestled between a set of laurels—just the essentials, streamlined and contained in a beautiful way.

It doesn't matter if we're organizing a closet, playroom, or refrigerator; our process always begins with a proper edit. So that's exactly what we're going to start before discussing the needs of specific spaces. Editing is a crucial part of the methodology that helps you fully assess your space and all the items it needs to accommodate. And the only way to understand the contents—and how best to organize them—is to make sure that anything you're about to make look really, really good is worth your time and energy.

Here's how the process looks at a glance:

1. TAKE EVERYTHING OUT
of the space you're organizing (and we mean *everything*).

2. CREATE GROUPINGS
by placing like items together so you can see what you're dealing with.

3. PARE DOWN
your belongings, getting rid of anything you no longer use or just don't like.

We know The Edit isn't everyone's favorite part. But, like going to the gym or eating your veggies, the process is good for you, even though it might suck at times and you might experience a range of emotions while going through your stuff. Editing is the foundation of a sustainable organized system. If you skip this piece because you're too excited about your trip to The Container Store or Target (we promise it won't be long before you get to push a cart down those aisles), you'll be doing yourself a disservice. By going through this process, you'll make room for the things you use and love and get rid of the things that have been holding you back from a perfectly organized home.

Embracing the LOW-BAR LIFESTYLE

The Low-Bar Lifestyle is a credo we came up with to describe just barely managing to make it through the day yet still feeling like you achieved something. It's something you can pat yourself on the back for and think, *Look at ME!* right before you pour yourself a drink and collapse on the couch. We apply the Low-Bar Lifestyle to all aspects of our life. If we give the kids a bath, then we get a gold star in parenting. If we microwave leftover pizza, another gold star. If we shower instead of putting our hair up in a bun, A-PLUS.

LOW-BAR LIFESTYLE RULES TO LIVE BY

Our general code of conduct looks like the following:

1. Applying heat to food is considered cooking.

2. A pizza is kind of a salad without lettuce . . . you've got cheese, tomatoes, and an extra big crouton. No shame in our pizza game!

3. Workout clothes are for every day, because getting through LIFE is a workout.

4. Champagne is basically sparkling water.

5. Trips to the store count as cardio.

It's all about setting the bar just low enough that you can accomplish all kinds of bite-size victories, because life is too short for feeling residual guilt about not wearing real pants or making it to the gym every day.

The same goes for organizing. Huge, daunting tasks are far too intimidating. Baby steps over a low, low, low bar will motivate you to keep on going. And since organizing is pretty much the only area in our lives where we set the bar very high, the good news is that we've done all the hard work for you. We're setting an easier standard for you so your project is accessible, attainable, and doable. Be patient with yourself and don't be afraid to give yourself plenty of gold stars for tackling smaller steps of a larger project.

One of the biggest pitfalls in organizing is choosing a project that's way too involved, starting it an hour before you have to pick your kids up from school, making an enormous mess of your house, and scrambling to stuff everything back where it came from. You'll find yourself swearing that you'll never ever do it again. If you follow our advice, we promise that won't happen.

It's all about staying motivated. Start with a smaller project, then take the confidence and knowledge you gain from that and apply it to a slightly larger project. We know you're fantasizing about all your dry goods in pretty jars—and they'll get there!—but first, be realistic about your time, experience, and abilities. There's no shame in starting small. In fact, the place we recommend beginning is with a single drawer.

That's right: **Start with a drawer.** It's pretty much the ideal space for getting your organizing feet wet. You follow the same exact steps of The Edit as you would for any other space, just in a bite-size way. Completely emptying out a drawer is a lot less daunting than emptying out a closet; you'll be able to see the light at the end of the tunnel much more quickly, and sorting through the contents will most likely be straightforward and uneventful. Then you can just tuck everything back in again and head to The Assembly on page 52 to see how best to organize the remaining items.

Feeling good? Move on to another space in your house and give it the same THE love!

Here's our guide to figuring out which projects tend to be easier and which generally take more time and effort:

EASY

A DRAWER

Choose any drawer! But start with *just one*. A single drawer is the best jumping-off point because it's small and manageable and will give you your first big win. We've included plenty of drawers in The Assembly section of the book, so take your pick! Personally, we are fans of the kitchen "junk" drawer since it gets used so often!

UNDER THE SINK

The dreaded under-the-sink area sounds (and might look) challenging, but it's actually very simple. And much like a drawer, it's contained and just takes the right inserts and configuration.

MEDIUM

THE BATHROOM

We still suggest biting off small sections at a time, but the bathroom presents pretty simple choices in a small space. Do you use the items? Are they empty or old? Just go through the motions of purging and containing, and you will get through this space with flying colors.

PLAY SPACES

Toys can feel like a big problem, but they don't have to be. If you consistently clear out the ones that aren't in regular use, have missing pieces, or have seen a better day, you will eliminate most of your workload. The bonus? You can donate the purged toys to a local shelter. The extra bonus? Cleaning up after your kids is the best cardio on the planet—the Low-Bar Lifestyle at its finest!

HARD

THE CLOSET

Tackling your closet can sometimes feel like climbing a mountain. And not just because it's physically challenging, but because it can be emotionally draining and complicated. Thoughts of *Will I ever fit into that dress again?* and *But what if I decide to have another child?* drift in and out of your head as you sift through the hangers. And that's okay. Refer to our "Rules for Getting Rid of Stuff" (page 41) to determine whether you should keep certain items, and give yourself a pass if you just aren't sure. Remember, we're setting the bar low. Just make it to the other side and raise it higher on another day.

THE KITCHEN AND PANTRY

In many ways, the pantry is the opposite of a clothing closet. There's nothing emotional about almond flour and cashews, so decision-making should come easily. The hard part about a pantry is that it's an enormous Rubik's Cube, and once it's pulled apart, it can be tedious to reassemble. The same can be true for a kitchen. So make sure to take stock of your space and have a plan of attack before you empty each shelf and drawer. There are a lot of kitchen and pantry examples in The Assembly; all you have to do is pick a space that most resembles your own and implement accordingly.

STEP 1:

TAKE IT *ALL* OUT

This is where you take the leap of faith. Are things about to get a little messy? Yes. Will you unearth items that give you minor twinges of chest pain? Quite possibly. Do you have to touch every single thing that lives in your drawer/cabinet/closet, pick it up, move it, and arrange it somewhere else? One hundred percent YES. This means that the space you're organizing should be completely empty by the time you're done. It's the only way you're going to find the dusty purses that have been shoved in the corner of the closet or the expired food in the back of your pantry.

If you leave anything inside the space, you're saying, "I basically eat all that food" or "I basically wear all those clothes," but we're here to tell you that that's the kind of thinking that got you into this mess in the first place. If you don't get in there and pull out every single item, then you're just kicking the can of beans down the road, not to mention building a faulty foundation with your organizing project. It's a lot more difficult to come up with an efficient *and* beautiful system if you have to accommodate items you don't care that much about. The purging part of the process comes later, but you can't effectively pare down if you don't know exactly what you have. Assessing each and every item, on the other hand, will help you figure out exactly what you still need/use/love, so you can get rid of the rest.

So clear off some space on your kitchen counter, bed, or bathroom floor, and strip those shelves and drawers until they are bare. And don't forget to wipe them down once they're empty . . . there's bound to be some dust and debris.

STEP 2:
CREATE GROUPINGS

As you're taking things out of your space, or after everything's already out, group your items into general categories: gym clothes, T-shirts, and jeans; or eye makeup, lipstick, and face wash. You don't need to worry about the organizing piece yet, just pair like items. For example, if you're cleaning out your fridge, group all the drinks together. You don't have to worry about whether the milk should be hanging out with the juice or sparkling water. Just stick with drinks.

This step helps with a couple of very important things. First, it keeps the project from devolving into a chaotic mess that makes you wish you never bought this book. Second, it will help you tremendously with the most difficult step: getting rid of anything you don't wear, use, or want. Instead of going through every item one by one, seeing things in natural groupings will give you a more holistic context for what you own. It will help you see where you have unnecessary duplicates (i.e., thirteen white T-shirts) and decide which items are worthy of keeping.

And we'll say this again: Don't be tempted to start organizing yet. We can't tell you how many times we've had to slap our own hands from putting fruit snacks into a jar right off the bat. We have to remind ourselves not to get carried away, too. If you attempt organization at this stage, you risk getting overwhelmed. We don't do it that way for a reason: It's way too hard. For now, avoid thinking about all the labels you're going to make and stick with this one task.

STEP 3:

PARE DOWN

Pour yourself an extra-generous glass of champagne (or if you're Team Joanna, a cup of tea). Because it's officially time to edit. Take a hard look at everything sitting in front of you and ask yourself, Are all these things worth my energy? That's really what this all comes down to—deciding which items are worth your attention, time, and effort when it comes to creating (and maintaining) a gorgeous, clean, Zen-like space that makes you happy every single day. We hereby give you permission to get rid of the things you don't use or love (or even like). So in case you need to tear this out and tape it on your fridge:

IT'S OKAY TO GET RID OF THINGS.

If you spot an item that is no longer serving you—physically or emotionally—it's okay to let it go. It's not doing you any favors. In fact, it's hogging precious space in your house and in your brain. We're willing to bet that every time you see that unused ice cream maker or fondue set (you will never have a fondue party), that unworn designer jacket your mother-in-law gave you, or that unopened bag of almond flour you bought for a recipe you never made, you feel a bit guilty. Or you had to spend some energy to plan for when you'd actually put that item to good use (which would never end up happening, leading you back to guilt—but maybe that's just us because we're two Jewish women raised by Jewish mothers, and guilt was the cornerstone of our upbringing).

Bottom line: It's FINE to get rid of things that are taking up space. No one will ask to see the scarf they gave you for Christmas or wonder where the dish towels with the Audrey Hepburn quotes are, or question why you never use the martini glasses you received for your wedding fifteen years ago. And if *you* bought yourself an item you never use, remember that we all make mistakes. Don't double down on the mistake by keeping it.

Here are our tips for low-stress, tears-free purging:

1. **Have bags on hand.** Buy a box of large black garbage bags. Designate some bags for trash, some for donations, and some for friends and family. It's essential to bag up your items as you're purging—the progress will help you stay motivated. Plus, it feels so satisfying to clear things off the floor or counter and into the bags rather than just moving them from pile to pile.

2. **Have a plan for what items you'll donate or give away.** Whether it's scheduling an appointment for a Salvation Army pickup or making a list of the people you want to give certain items to, knowing the exit strategy for these things strongly decreases the likelihood that your giveaway bags will still be sitting in your trunk a year from now. Be realistic when coming up with your plan—are you really going to schlep fifteen unopened wedding gifts to the UPS Store so you can individually ship them? And that bag of clothes you plan on selling online . . . are you *really* going to sell them or just let them sit in a garbage bag graveyard until you forget they exist anyway? If you think you might need some hand-holding in this department, enlist a friend to help!

3. **Have a small (small!) project pile.** A watch with a missing link, an iPad with a cracked screen, a jacket that needs to be altered—these things can go in their own "special attention" pile. Fix them (sooner rather than later) and then move them back into their newly renovated home.

4. **Consider the storing or archiving option.** For some items, a binary choice—keep or throw out—isn't appropriate. These are things you still want in your house but don't need to look at all the time or have within arm's reach. Your tax returns don't need to sit on your desk, but they should be filed away safely in an appropriate place. Sentimental items can be packed away in the attic or basement instead of taking up valuable real estate in a living-room cabinet. Heavy winter clothes don't need to be front and center in your closet in the summertime, so maybe they go in a seasonal bin on a shelf that you need a step stool to reach.

5. **Just keep moving.** Once you get into an editing groove, don't give up and say you'll come back to it another time. Stopping and restarting is a big reason people tend to lose interest and confidence when tackling an organizing project. Think of it like running (not that we know much about running, but this seems like a good metaphor): If you're training for a 5K but you let two weeks go by between each run, it's like you're starting from scratch every time. We can't urge you enough to take advantage of the motivation to make a change in your home, harness that momentum, and hang on for dear life. What will go a long way is making sure you give yourself plenty of time for The Edit. You can always come back later for the organizing piece, but make sure you can get through The Edit in one session. This comes back to not biting off more than you can chew, an essential rule for pain-free organizing and one that we'll help you navigate later in this chapter.

6. **Take one more pass.** Before moving on to the next steps, take another look at all the items you have left. Make sure every single thing is worth the time and energy it'll take to physically put it back in your space. If you feel great, then fantastic! You've officially completed the editing process. Pat yourself on the back and take a breath. The rest of our methodology is *way* more fun.

THE RULES *for Getting Rid of Stuff*

As you go through your things, ask yourself these questions. If it helps to visualize us hovering over you, that's totally fine and not weird at all.

1. **Do I need it?** Some things are just a part of life and will stay with us for better or worse. We don't really *love* our toaster ovens, but we aren't going to get rid of them. So if you need it, it can stay.

2. **Do I ever use it?** EVER? Even once a year? A good example would be a roasting pan. You might use it only on Thanksgiving, but at least you can confirm that you *do* use it, even if infrequently.

3. **Do I ever WANT to use it?** This question usually applies to things like ice cream makers, fondue sets, and workout equipment. We all have good intentions, but we also have a limited amount of space. So try to picture yourself making ice cream before just buying a pint at the grocery store instead. Yeah, we didn't think so.

4. **Do I like it?** Answer honestly. If you do honestly like it, then keep it. You get a full pass for things that make you happy. If you don't like it, answer question number 2 before getting rid of it.

5. **Is it sentimental?** If the answer is yes, consider just how sentimental it is. Is it *your-child made-you-a-piece-of-pottery-at-someone's-birthday-party* type of sentimental, or is it *your-grandmother's-china-that-you-don't-like-but-you're-going-to-give-it-to-your-daughter-one-day-so-it-becomes-her-problem* type of sentimental? (If you're reading this, Roberta, Clea LOVES Grandma Nancy's china and, um, can't wait for Stella to inherit it.) Depending on whether you deem the item worthy of sentimental attachment, you can make the decision about whether it should be donated or properly stored. It's okay to hold on to something you care about EVEN if you don't really like it, as long as it's not taking up valuable real estate in your home. Utilize the top shelves in your closet; the attic, basement, or garage; or even a storage unit, if needed. Just don't let these items take up your everyday living space, since they don't serve your everyday needs.

Shopping THE *Way*

We can't stress enough to ALWAYS take stock of your space before you start organizing. This will help you account for all of your items and better understand the parameters of the space itself. During this process, make sure to take photos of your space so you can refer back to them at the store. If you try to make a mental note of everything you have, and how many shelves you need to fill, you will be making multiple shopping trips for everything you missed. Here are some tried-and-true tips:

- **Measure your space:** the height, width, length, and depth. To source the right product, you need to know your dimensions down to the quarter inch. Be sure to write down detailed information, such as the shelf depth, height between shelves, and drawer depth and height.

- **Maximize your usable space** by selecting products that will take the best advantage of each shelf. Once you understand which pieces *fit* the best, you can look at your options and determine the aesthetic you prefer.

- **Consider the negative space options** as well. For instance, do you want to use the floor to create extra storage or keep it clean and open? Do you want to take advantage of door space or leave it open?

- **Don't be afraid to shop the *entire* store** for any given space. You might find the perfect item for your kitchen in the bathroom section (hello, toilet paper holder).

- **ALWAYS buy containers in a variety of sizes.** We routinely leave the store with twenty-eight shopping bags in tow, but we swear there is a method to the madness. You have to give yourself options while organizing because, inevitably, the product that you thought would be *perfect* doesn't always work as well as you hoped. Not a problem! Just keep trying your backup product until you find the one that works best.

- **Buy in bulk!** You will always need a larger quantity than you think, so purchase extra containers and return the overage.

- **Consider your lifestyle.** When shopping for organizational products you have to realistically consider your day-to-day routine and who lives in your household. Are you someone who has the time or energy to come home from the grocery store and empty each cereal box into a canister, or is a big bin for cereal boxes an easier and more sustainable solution? Do you have a system in place for finding all of the little items you tuck in to storage boxes lined up on your bookshelves so you don't lose track? There is no wrong way to get organized as long as you can commit to the long-term maintenance.

- **Consistency is key,** so try to buy storage containers in the same collection or at least the same color. Matching products instantly elevate a space, while mismatched products can make it look sloppy. Streamlining your supplies will make everything look polished.

STORAGE ITEMS *We Can't Live Without*

Keep a lookout for these items at your local home goods store:

SHOE BOXES: Not the cardboard boxes from your shopping trip. The ones we like are plastic with snap-on lids to keep items dust-free. You can use them for shoes, but they have other great uses as well. Also, the see-through plastic is ideal for storing seasonal items (so you can remember what you've stored).

LAZY SUSANS: Not just for spice cabinets—you can also use these for crafts, toiletries, laundry supplies, and under the kitchen sink. Just to name a few!

STORAGE INSERTS: Go for the unlidded kind for easy access and fast pickup like in kids' playrooms where you need to organize things quickly and neatly. Or use them on closet shelves for organizing small accessories and sunglasses. These can tip over (and they're not lidded) so make sure they're lined up safely and on a stable surface, like on a shelf with a lip.

NONSLIP HANGERS: No wire hangers! JK, but seriously, why bother hanging things up if they just slip off and fall on the floor? Velvety hangers are a godsend—they'll hold anything.

DOOR RACKS: The inside of every closet or pantry should have a door rack, and a quick search online shows so many different uses: for organizing shoes, gift wrap, the tops of pots and pans. If you haven't shopped for a door rack lately, you're missing out.

MAGAZINE FILES: We almost never use magazine files for their intended purpose. Instead, we put them to use separating handbags, clutches, notebooks, stationery, board games, and boxed puzzles.

STORAGE BASKETS WITH HANDLES: Handled baskets are one of our most frequently used items. They serve the critical purpose of containment and allow for easy-to-reach access on upper shelves.

CLEAR PANTRY BINS: Nothing goes in our refrigerator or freezer without first being stashed in a clear bin. They're great for avoiding spills and organizing types of food.

LINED STORAGE BINS: Don't put delicate items in bins that will snag. Look for lined baskets. Also, they add a softer touch for the bedroom.

STORAGE TIERS: Make your pantry shelves work a little harder with these tiered shelves, which help you reach the back of the cabinet more easily.

Our SIGNATURE LOOK

Here's the good news: After you edit everything down and go shopping, the hard part is over, and the actual organizing can now commence. Because, as the saying goes, good things come to those who group and categorize appropriately and don't just skip to the end. Here is the method behind our madness.

FORM AND FUNCTION *Are Equals*

One of the reasons we strive to make spaces as aesthetically pleasing as possible is because we know how powerful a motivator that can be for a client to keep it looking that way. The truth is, people are more willing to commit to something if it feels good *and* it looks good. It's like how when you finally get in shape, you're motivated to keep it up. You just need to remind yourself, *Hey, you already did all the hard work; you already made a system for making this change—now you just have to maintain it*. Except instead of early-morning cardio and eating nothing but yogurt, the *only* thing you have to commit to is putting the cereal in the Breakfast bin. So much easier! Regardless of whether it's toned-up arms or a meticulously organized playroom, it would be sad to see all that hard work go to waste.

   To be clear, though, when we talk about maintenance, we're not saying that your space needs to be photo-ready 100 percent of the time. Even our homes aren't that hard core! Not every one of our drawers and closets is going to be perfectly beautiful at all moments—but they are going to be really good at all times, because (a) allowing for a breakdown in the system is a very slippery slope—and when it falls off the cliff a little bit, it falls off a lot—and (b) surrounding ourselves with attractive, well-organized spaces makes us really, really happy.

RAINBOW *Is* BRIGHT

One of our signatures that sets our spaces apart from other organizers' is our affinity for ROYGBIV (Red, Orange, Yellow, Green, Blue, Indigo, Violet, for those who need a refresher), or sorting items by color and organizing them by the spectrum of the rainbow. This is partially a design decision—things in rainbow order are pleasing to the eye—but it's also an organizational tool. Our brains innately recognize this pattern, making it a natural scheme for making sense of where we put things.

      Whether it's drugstore items, soft drink cans, bags of snack foods, LEGOs, or T-shirts, if you display items in rainbow order, it creates a visual flow that naturally clicks with the brain. It makes it faster to find what you're looking for and easier for you to know where things should be put away, and it's certainly gentler on the eyes than any other method. It's part of what makes our systems so user-friendly—because sometimes you're not the only one using them. For kids, this method not only helps them know exactly where to put things away, but it also inspires them creatively. Suddenly, cleanup is less a chore and more of a sorting challenge or game. So we promise you, there really is logic to the rainbow, and it perfectly sums up the marriage of aesthetic and function.

LABEL, LABEL, LABEL

The other, literal, signature that makes our work unique is our labeling. But contrary to the belief that this finishing touch is frosting on the organizational cake, we believe that this is actually the secret to long-term maintenance. The key to keeping up a system isn't so much the containers you choose—although that's critical—but the labeling. The labels, whether they're handwritten, typed, needlepointed, whatever, are really a set of instructions. Just as how ROYGBIV is an intuitive blueprint (and is a type of labeling in and of itself), clearly and concretely identifying the contents that belong in a container gives you, your kids, your partner, your houseguests, and anyone else using the space straightforward directions for where items go.

When items stay where they belong, you're successfully maintaining an organizational system. That's why it's so important that you get the labeling right. It has to hit the sweet spot between the general and the specific, and it should be the perfect assortment of categories so that when you put away your groceries, laundry, or newest stash of crafting supplies, you barely have to think about it. What you want is a simple road map that's flexible enough to allow for the occasional outlier. What you *don't* want are overly specific containers that lock you in, so you find yourself sticking things anywhere because it's better than nowhere and then the system starts to fall apart and the sky opens up and all hell breaks loose and you're left with total anarchy. We can't have that weighing on our conscience, so here are some things to consider before you take out the paint pen.

Think about your general categories *before* your specific ones. The general categories will be much larger groupings: for instance, "Breakfast" in a pantry. But if you notice you have a significant amount of oatmeal, you can create a specific category just for oatmeal. Or in a bathroom, you might have a large amount of hair products in general, but also a wide selection of just dry shampoos (ahem, Low-Bar Lifestyle). In that case, you could have a general bin labeled "Hair Supplies" and another bin labeled and devoted exclusively to "Dry Shampoo." What you want to avoid is having all specific bins, because inevitably you will buy something, bring it home, and have no idea where it goes. Our rule of thumb is to always lean toward general categories because you can't go wrong. More granular categories should be secondary.

Here are some examples of general and specific labels for various parts of the house. There's no right or wrong label—it's just important that all things are accounted for!

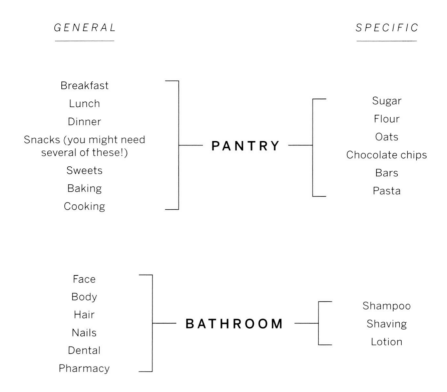

GENERAL

SPECIFIC

Breakfast
Lunch
Dinner
Snacks (you might need several of these!)
Sweets
Baking
Cooking

PANTRY

Sugar
Flour
Oats
Chocolate chips
Bars
Pasta

Face
Body
Hair
Nails
Dental
Pharmacy

BATHROOM

Shampoo
Shaving
Lotion

TOP 5 LABELS WE'VE CREATED

1. Jewish Stuff + Magic Tricks (nothing will ever top that one!)

2. Babies, Bibs, and Butts

3. Wig glitter and weave parts

4. Stuff I have to keep

5. Aspirational denim

GENERAL

SPECIFIC

Shirts
Tanks
Hats
Bags
Unmentionables
Pajamas
Seasonal
Shoes

CLOSET

Sports bras
Workout shorts
Clutches
Sweatpants
Swim

Blocks/Building
Dolls/Figurines
Games
Animals
Crafts
Sports

PLAYROOM

Barbies
Disney characters
Magna-Tiles
LEGOs
Kitchen equipment
Play food
Tools
Magic set
Wands

Laundry
Cleaning
Ironing
Utility
Household

LAUNDRY ROOM

Detergent
Dryer sheets
Fabric softener
Borax
Lightbulbs

Entertaining
Outdoor
Holidays
Sentimental
Winter
Summer
Kids

STORAGE

Platters
Towels
Halloween decorations
Beach toys

the assembly

W hen we first approached writing this book, we started thinking about it like a cookbook (which is admittedly ironic, because we do not cook). Nonetheless, it felt like an appropriate analogy: We wanted to give you a collection of organizing recipes alongside inspiring photographs, in the hopes that if you follow those instructions, you'll achieve similar results.

For this recipe book, we wanted to show you how to assemble spaces in your home the same way that we do. You might not get a casserole at the end, but you *will* reclaim your sanity and your household. We're going to cover a lot of ground in this section and work our way through the entire house, but do not get overwhelmed. Rome was not built in a day, and it wasn't organized in a day, either. The purpose of showing you a range of spaces, with different aesthetics, at varying degrees of difficulty, is to help you pull together inspiration for your own home when you're ready to embark on the challenge. And if you need to stick to the bunny slope for a while, you can organize every drawer in the house until you're ready to tackle a larger space and still find great peace of mind. Always keep in mind our mantra about the Low-Bar Lifestyle (see page 26), and you'll be fine. Remember: Baby steps are small victories. And leggings *are* pants.

ENTRY

Let's start with the entryway, which is a space that varies quite a bit from home to home. For some, it might mean a mudroom; for others, it might mean a coat closet by the front door. But what we all have in common is that every one of us enters our home through a door and needs a place where we can immediately put down our things. Even the smallest New York City apartment needs a hook on the wall or a tiny table for keys and mail.

Take stock of all the items that enter and exit your house on a daily basis. This might include backpacks, coats, hats, handbags, umbrellas, mail, keys, etc.—but each household has varying categories. Then take a moment to think about where everything naturally lands when you walk in the door. For instance, do shoes pile up on the floor? Does mail end up on the kitchen counter? Once you've figured out everything you need to account for, design a solution that will fit your needs *and* your space.

TOP 5 WAYS TO KEEP YOUR ENTRY LOOKING PICTURE PERFECT AT ALL TIMES

1. Live alone.

2. Make sure your kids use a separate entrance.

3. Don't own things.

4. Change your mailing address to your neighbors' and pick up your mail once a week.

5. Start going places without shoes or jackets so there's nothing to take off when you walk in the door.

Or . . . just accept that it won't stay perfect ALL the time, but cleaning up counts as cardio.

THE MAKESHIFT ENTRY

Some entryways only have room for a table and not much else. The trick is to maximize the space in every way possible so that all your categories stay organized. Within just three square feet, we created an easy-to-maintain system for a family of four.

1. Decorative objects on the tabletop preempt any pileup of coats and handbags (these items belong hung on hooks or in a nearby closet)

2. A table with drawers designated for mail, keys, and sunglasses

3. A divided and labeled basket underneath the table holds backpacks (one per child) and hanging files

THE TRADITIONAL MUDROOM

A standard mudroom generally has three or four built-in stalls and includes hooks and cubbies, which is the equivalent of an organizational blank canvas. A mudroom can *also* be the equivalent of Grand Central Terminal, so it's a good idea to designate a spot for each member of the family. It will hold everyone accountable for his or her own space!

1. Seasonal and infrequently used items placed in baskets on harder-to-access upper shelves

2. A hook for each family member

3. Knit hats and mittens for the winter and hats and sunscreen for the summer stored in lower lidded bins

4. Shoe baskets for each child (clearly labeled!)

MOLLY SIMS'S MUDROOM

Molly Sims's mudroom is another example of a traditional setup—although the cushioned seating and high-gloss lacquered paint make it much more glam than most! The organization principles, however, remain the same as for the last mudroom: hooks for each member of the family and baskets for the remaining categories.

1. Extra towels and bulky items stored in upper cabinets

2. Outdoor supplies are accessible and easy to grab on the way out the door

3. After-school sports and activities have designated baskets

4. Two shoe baskets for each child provide ample storage for the whole family

ENTRY

THE
BEACHY
MUDROOM

Every now and then we get to put a fun twist on an old standard. A mudroom at the beach would technically be more of a sandroom . . . Instead of accounting for hats and mittens, you just have to account for sunscreen and goggles.

1. Extra straw hats and rolled beach towels to grab on the way to the beach

2. Bins for outdoor sprays and sunscreens, extra hats, sunglasses, and beach supplies

3. Lightweight baskets for shoes on the bottom shelf

TIP/   Coordinate the hats and towels you leave out for guests to give your space extra style.

1
lightbulbs
utility
2
3
Clea
Clea
Stella
Stella
Stella
4
Winter
Summer
John
John
Sutton
Sutton
Sutton

THE MULTIPURPOSE CLOSET

We like to take *full* advantage of every square inch of storage. If you have a front hall closet or a storage closet, consider all the categories you might be able to store in it. In this case, we fit coats, shoes, rain gear, pharmacy, and utility items by creating zones for each category.

1. Extra utility and household items line the top shelf

2. Pharmacy, wellness, and first-aid products visibly stored in clear bins

3. Two or three pairs of shoes for each member of the family

4. Summer and winter items in floor baskets

TIP/ If you have kids, it's a good idea to keep adult medications on a higher shelf and leave safer items like bandages within their reach!

THE COAT CLOSET

Just because it's a coat closet doesn't mean it has to hold only coats. As long as the items stay contained and labeled, they are free to crash the coat party. In this case, we needed to store outdoor items and extra entertaining supplies close to the back door so they'd be accessible for the deck, and the coat closet was the perfect solution.

1. Opaque bins to conceal loose entertaining supplies

2. Overstock of supplies lined behind the bins

3. Sturdy hangers used for heavy coats

Outdoor   Outdoor

soap

aprons

Booties

Dance

Soccer

Karate

1

2

3

4

5

6

CHRISTINA APPLEGATE'S MUDROOM

Christina's mudroom shows off her supermom status. Yes, she has a busy career, but she still manages to remember snacks for soccer games. We told her we'd be happy to organize all the dance bags, karate uniforms, and soccer cleats if she could *please* give us mom lessons.

1. Convenient pharmacy and first-aid station without taking up space in the kitchen

2. Hats on hooks

3. Uniforms and activity bags stored in lightweight bins with handles that are easy for kids to access

4. Bins of extra water bottles to snatch before leaving the house

5. Clean countertop for incoming mail and packages

6. Shoes in individual cubbies and off the floor

TIP/ Store your heaviest appliances on low shelves—it's more practical, and safer!

LAUNDRY

We're not big fans of doing laundry, but organizing a laundry room is our idea of a good time (that said, we're experts on organization, NOT experts on fun, so take this with a grain of salt). Laundry rooms are near the top of our list of favorite spaces to organize for a few reasons:

1. Whether you live alone or have a large family, it's a constantly used space, and it greatly benefits from functionality. And as organizing nerds, we LOVE getting to help with that transformation.

2. Small changes and minimal products go a long way to transform the space.

3. Alleviating the headache of the laundry *room* makes the chore of doing laundry slightly better. Sort of. We still don't like it.

Some people go to great lengths to have a laundry room that's out of a magazine page, and others just keep it tucked off in a corner of the house. Truthfully, we like both scenarios. If the space is beautifully designed, we like to enhance the aesthetic with equally designed functionality. And if the space is a bare-bones eyesore, we'll transform it into something as practical as it is Instagram-worthy.

Before embarking on your laundry room redo, consider the categories you want to store. Obviously you will have detergent, but what about stain removal, dryer sheets, and other cleaners? Do you need space for rags and towels? Should you leave room for folding clothes, or do you do that elsewhere? Thinking through your categories and laundry process will help you set up a plan of attack. Even if that plan changes, it will give you a jumping-off point!

THE ESSENTIALS CABINET

Admit it—this kind of looks like a good time, right? Bright white bins of sprays and detergent and an easy-to-grab bin for ironing create a super-simple setup and a clean and crisp design.

1. Sponges in small, easy-to-remove containers

2. Oversize black labels to contrast with the white bins

3. Plastic bins with handles that can be easily wiped down

4. Large containers of detergents made to fit after adjusting shelf height

TIP/ Don't shy away from a label, and when you can, make it big and bold!

Ironing

Cleaning

LAUNDRY

THE
NO-STORAGE
LAUNDRY ROOM

Sometimes, a beautiful room in a beautiful home can lack in functionality. This laundry room was sleek and stylish, but it didn't have a single shelf or cabinet. Nothing a good basket can't solve! Just utilize the counter or top of the washing machine, and your storage problem is solved.

1. Laundry supplies, utility items, and gift wrap placed in extra-large baskets

2. Detergents and specialty cleaners lined up on a tray

3. Remaining space reserved for folding clothes

THE SINGLE SHELF LAUNDRY ROOM

Hey, one shelf is better than no shelf. You just need to put that shelf to good use! Both of these spaces have laundry, cleaning, and outdoor supplies—so we used a similar approach to store the categories in each home.

1. Detergent and laundry pods in lidded jars add a luxe look at very little cost, AND you can easily see when it's time to restock

2. Everyday cleaning and laundry items in open bins for easy access

3. Extra household supplies and sunscreen in concealed lidded bins

TIP/ Using stackable storage means the sky is the limit—literally! Stack as high as you're able to and gain valuable extra space!

THE GIANT UTILITY ROOM

Not everyone has a laundry room that can hold a high school dance, but if you're one of the lucky ones who does have one, you're going to want to keep all those cabinets and drawers organized, especially when you're storing more than just laundry supplies. Otherwise, it can easily turn into the room equivalent of a junk drawer.

1. Laundry supplies, household items, and tools organized into upper cabinets

2. Clean counter accommodates folding sheets and towels

3. Dog biscuits displayed in a counter canister

4. Industrial-size laundry hampers on wheels are ideal for large homes since they make gathering and sorting laundry easier

THE ENDLESS LOADS OF LAUNDRY CABINET

Doing lots and lots of laundry for a big family is kind of . . . terrible. But imagine a world where you enjoy a little moment of Zen every time you open the cabinet to grab the detergent. We're not saying that feeling will last beyond the spin cycle, but every little bit helps!

1. Labeled containers separate splurge-worthy specialty products from stain removers

2. Enamel container and stainless steel scoop elevate humble powder detergent

3. Liquid detergents line the bottom shelf for easy access

DOS AND DON'TS IN A LAUNDRY ROOM

DO use bins that can be wiped out easily when the liquid detergent inevitably spills.

DO NOT use decorative woven baskets, unless you want them permanently stained blue.

DO use a canister for laundry pods and ditch the plastic container they came in.

DO NOT store detergent in other rooms of the house, because that would make zero sense.

DO store items from around the house in the laundry room.

- DENTAL -

- BACKSTOCK -

1

2

3

- DIAPERS -

- DIAPERS -

4

THE BACK STOCK CABINET

Very rarely do laundry rooms hold *only* laundry items. More often than not, the shelves and cabinets provide storage for extras from lightbulbs and batteries to dog food and baby supplies. As long as you keep your categories contained and labeled, anything is fair game.

1. Extra dental- and personal-care items organized into bins

2. Rolls of wrapped toilet paper stay dust-free when lined up on the shelf

3. Shelves adjusted to help take better advantage of the vertical space

4. Bins stocked with opened diapers allow for quick changes downstairs

TIP/ Removing excess packaging when you get home from the store makes your items more immediately accessible and infinitely better-looking in your bins.

THE DON'T-FORGET-THE-DOOR SOLUTION

We really, REALLY like using the door for extra storage. It always feels like a magic trick because you get to store more things without them taking up additional space. You will *also* probably notice in this book that we get really excited about things that might be questionable on the excitement scale—but such is the life of a professional organizer. Space and storage just get our blood flowing.

1. Overstocked items stay at the top since they don't need to be constantly accessible

2. Smaller items like sponges and rags organized into short door baskets

3. Sprays and cleaning solutions fit perfectly in deep door baskets

4. Baskets labeled for each cleaning category and room type

THE OPEN SHELF SOLUTION

Open shelving can be tricky in any scenario because you're forced to keep it looking good at all times. It can be even trickier when the shelves in question are located in a frequently used area like the laundry room. Since you don't have the luxury of closing the cabinet door, make sure that nothing is free-floating on the shelf, and it will stay looking neat at all times.

1. Entertaining extras stored nicely in handled bins for carrying to wherever they're needed

2. Often used household and utility supplies organized into stackable clear bins

3. Cleaning and laundry items stored in open bins for easy access, but the opaque design helps hide unsightly packaging

4. Frequently worn-and-washed sports uniforms organized into separate bin

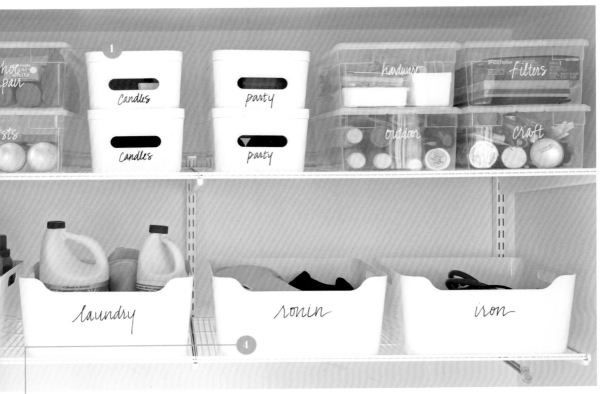

TIP/ Clear stackable storage is a great way to see the items you use most and access them easily. These bins are lightweight and stack securely, and you can identify all the contents with or without a label (but . . . you know how we feel about labeling, so add one anyway, okay?).

KAREN FAIRCHILD'S LAUNDRY ROOM

Without a doubt, one of the most beautiful laundry rooms we've ever been in belongs to Karen Fairchild from the country music group Little Big Town, and it was designed by the super-talented Rachel Halvorson. What we love even more than the stunning space is that it really functions as a multipurpose room. There's desk space, counters for folding, drawers for gift wrap, and cabinets for utility supplies. Artwork hanging on the wall adds inspiration so you don't feel isolated from the rest of the home while doing the wash. It's basically a laundry room dream come true.

1. Labeled hampers for everyone in the family

2. File boxes on the desk keep important documents neat and within reach

3. Closed cabinet bins keep laundry supplies out of the way when not in use

BATHROOM

Bathrooms are another one of our favorite rooms to organize. And I know you're thinking that we say *every* room is our favorite, but it's not true. Garages, basements, and attics: not so great. But a bathroom is SO FUN, and the possibilities are endless. Another nice thing about working on a bathroom is that the categories are pretty clear and generally consistent from home to home. You will almost always be organizing your items into these groupings:

> **FACE**
> **HAIR**
> **DENTAL**
> **BATH + BODY**

And likely some or all of these additional groupings:

> **EYE**
> **MAKEUP**
> **HAIR TOOLS**
> **COTTON SWABS AND ROUNDS**
> **BACK STOCK SUPPLIES**
> **TRAVEL**

And depending on your space and time constraints, you'll probably end up creating groupings *within* all these groupings. For instance, your makeup category might turn into subsections for blush, lip, and eye. These extra steps are always optional, so don't overwhelm yourself and bite off more than you can chew. If you can manage to get your basic categories grouped and organized, but you don't have the energy to sort them further, that is STILL a huge win. Fine-tune things later on—you'd be amazed at how easy it is to separate dry shampoo from hair spray while holding a glass of wine!

THE
SKIN SAVING
CABINET

Medicine cabinets seem to hold a lot more than pills these days. Since these cabinets are often prime real estate in the bathroom, they tend to be used for products and supplies that you reach for on a daily basis. For this non-medicine medicine cabinet, we created a dedicated spot for everyday face regimens.

1. Categories are grouped into cleansers, moisturizers, and treatments

2. Excess packaging removed to fit treatment packets in a space-saving drawer, so additional face masks can stack on top

3. Divided containers help to separate more specific subcategories

TIP/ It's always important to measure your spaces before buying products, but a medicine cabinet is trickier than most! Pay close attention to the depth of each shelf and the door hinges that might get in the way of your containers.

THE
SKIN SAVING
DRAWER

If your bathroom lacks cabinet space, you can just as easily use a drawer! Almost all bottles can lie flat as opposed to standing upright—just make sure lids are on extra tight to avoid an oil spill.

1. Odd-shaped chargers and other tools anchor the corner to maximize countertop space

2. Products are grouped by brand rather than category to keep sets together

3. Q-tips and cotton swabs separated into compartmented containers

TIP/ Drawer inserts don't just help with organization—they also protect your drawer from products that might leak or spill.

THE
NO-DRAWER
BATHROOM

If you have a bathroom without drawers, you can add additional storage by using wall units or freestanding carts. Both options bring functionality *and* unique design elements, so it's a fun twist for a standard bathroom setup. Plus, it's really fun wheeling your cart around when you need to restock items (don't knock it till you've tried it).

1. Bath and body supplies organized into the iron wall unit

2. Candles and decorative objects added to make the room more inviting

3. Folded towels and rolls of toilet paper fill the acrylic cart

THE
DAILY
DRAWER

Think of your "daily" drawer as the bathroom's greatest hits. These are the go-to items that you use twice a day without fail: toothbrush and toothpaste, contact lenses, face wipes—whatever suits your daily routine. In this instance, the daily drawer also doubles as a back stock drawer. When you need a new razor or toothbrush, it is right there waiting for you.

1. Bulky face wipes are organized without containers, but they help secure the categories on either side

2. Categories are separated with modular drawer organizers in varying sizes

3. Items used together are next to each other in the drawer

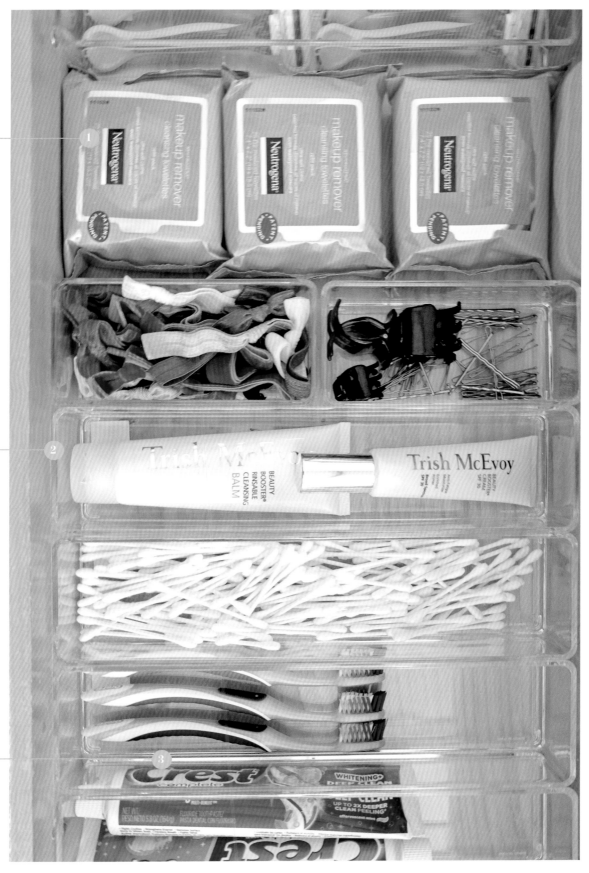

EVERYTHING AND THE BATHROOM SINK

The space beneath the bathroom sink is just as important as the storage under the kitchen sink and should not be ignored. In many instances, it's the best place to stand up large bottles of shampoo, hair products, lotion, and more, so put it to good use!

1. Extra pull-out deep drawers to take advantage of the cabinet depth

2. Back stock of hair, face, and makeup products organized into separate containers

3. Cup inserts used in the makeup drawer keep small items from rolling around

LINEN CLOSET
OPEN SHELVING

In theory, folded linens and towels would look perfect on an open shelf. Alas, there's the inconvenient truth that you don't live in a hotel or spa (YET . . . there's always hope), and it's not ever going to look as pristine when you try to replicate the stack of towels in your own home. But with the help of a few baskets, you'll get the look and save your sanity.

1. Extra toilet paper rolls stacked in rows

2. Transparent baskets for easy-to-see categories

3. Folded towels, hand towels, and washcloths stay neatly contained

TIP/ Toilet paper can be stored in a floor basket if a nearby shelf isn't available—but buy wrapped rolls to keep them from getting dusty!

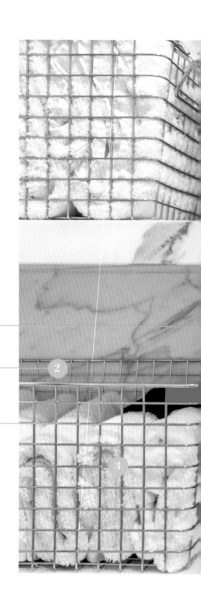

THE PRETTY STOCKPILE SHELF

Open shelving is usually reserved for things that are meant to be displayed, like dishes or books. Extra bathroom products, on the other hand, are usually stashed out of sight, hidden behind cabinet doors and drawers. But adding some elevated products and clean categories can make all the difference in this room!

1. Clear bins on upper shelves store neatly contained, unopened back stock items

2. Bulky face and hair care products stored in concealed bins to mask the contents

3. Prettier items like nail polish and a manicure kit stored in take-along caddies

TIP/ Whenever possible, try to pick bins that line up flush with the edge of the shelf. It creates a custom look that visually improves the space (regardless of what is stored inside!).

GUEST BATHROOM DRAWER

Setting up a guest bathroom is fun because you can include things you wouldn't use yourself on a daily basis. Whether it's fancy toothpaste or some luxury toiletries, you can splurge knowing these are not everyday items.

1. Bath and body products lined up behind the drawer organizers to hold everything in place

2. ROYGBIV-arranged toothpaste in travel sizes

3. Compartmentalized dental and face supplies

TIP/ A guest bathroom drawer can be a great place to practice your organizing skills! It's pretty low-risk (unless you have a particular mother named Roberta) since it's not used every day, so you can't go wrong!

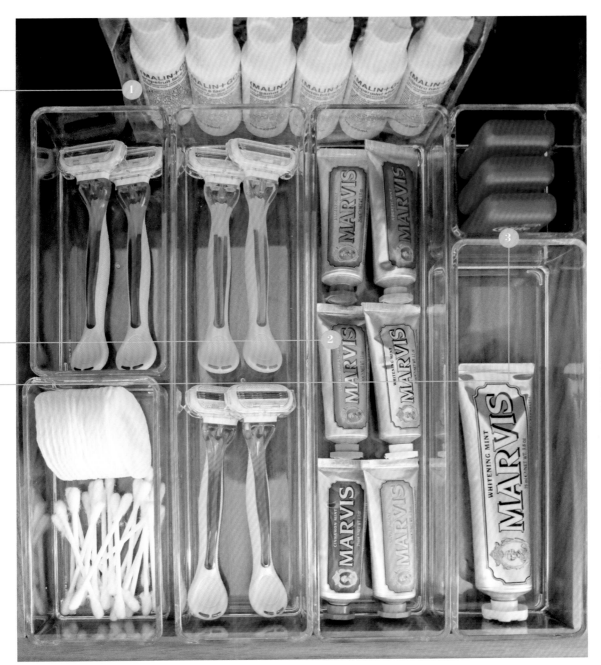

THE ASSEMBLY ❧ 107

COUNTERTOP STORAGE

Some people prefer to keep their makeup on the counter where they can see it, and some people *need* to make use of the countertop because they are short on storage space. If you fall into either of those buckets, stackable acrylic containers might change your life. Okay, maybe not your *life*, but certainly your bathroom.

1. Makeup can be kept in this single tower or broken up into a different configuration, and individual sections can be removed while items are in use

2. Face, eye, and lip products categorized and contained in modular acrylic drawers in varying sizes for a custom fit

3. Products lined up in each drawer to keep the color label visible whenever possible

BATHROOM
SUPPLY
CABINET

If you're lucky enough to have a storage closet in your bathroom, add storage bins that keep your items front and center. Once your spray bottles and first-aid supplies are neatly organized, you won't mind looking at them!

1. Pharmacy and first-aid products organized on a turntable and in under-shelf organizers

2. Boxes removed from capsules with visible names and dosages marked on the interior packaging

3. Cleaning supplies are organized on a turntable, with toilet paper stacked neatly on either side to fill out the space

TIP/ Sometimes you need to think outside the bin . . .Under-shelf organizers help hold items you need easy access to, AND they are uniquely able to take full vertical advantage of your shelves.

STOCKED
BY SCENT

Sometimes when we are organizing a space, a *very* specific theme will emerge, and we realize that it is a stand-alone category. In this case, among the cleansers and lotions, we noticed that the scents definitely deserved their own labels: grapefruit, orange, and coconut. And isn't it a little bit more fun to have a grapefruit grouping? Everything deserves its own moment to shine, even citrus-scented bath products.

1. Small cabinet bins divide each category of small items

2. Stacked bins on the top shelf take advantage of the height

3. A middle shelf used to store the most compact items helps maximize space on the other shelves

4. Categories grouped by scent rather than type so you can match a fragrance to your mood

BATHROOM

THE BUT-WAIT-THERE'S-MORE CABINET

What do you do when you think you nailed your categories but then discover there's actually more where those came from? Behold, the back stock cabinet. And this extra stock was extra-satisfying because it helped underscore our firm commitment to the scent-based categories we chose for the bathroom's *other* cabinet (see page 113).

1. A nail station sits on the shelf above (never miss your chance to arrange polish in a rainbow), with nail supplies in the drawer below

2. A scent category for practicality (and personal victory)

3. Tall bath and body products are able to stand upright in modular drawers in varying sizes

TIP/ When you want clear storage for visibility, but maybe don't want all your personal items on display, a frosted clear helps achieve both goals.

① coconut + orange

② nail

grapefruit

③ body + hand

HOME OFFICE

Home offices are *sometimes* really enjoyable to work on, and sometimes . . . they are not. That's usually because we never know what we're going to get with a client's office, since each one is so different. Some offices have a ton of files and paper, some are for crafting and gift wrapping, and some are for home businesses that operate out of a single room. And still others have documents dating back decades (ahem, those are not the fun ones). So when we are gearing up to organize an office, we approach it with trepidation, then either breathe a sigh of relief or brace ourselves for the long day ahead.

That said, we're going to show you the ones we are most proud to have organized to help you declutter your own workspace. And since every office is so uniquely different, we encourage you to take bits and pieces of inspiration from some of these projects and stitch them together to fit your home's needs.

THE JEWELRY STUDIO

Here's a tip: If you ever find yourself organizing seven million tiny beads, charms, and crystals the size of quinoa (surely we aren't the only people who find ourselves in such predicaments), do NOT, under any circumstance, dump the beads on a cookie sheet for sorting. They will magnetize together and form some kind of DNA double helix, and there is nothing you can do to turn back the hands of time and unwind the mess you've made.

But after three days of sorting beads smaller than grains of sand, everything came together beautifully, and we were so proud of the outcome. We were also grateful that we were all still speaking, because it was touch and go for a bit.

1. Decorative boxes on the top shelf used for sentimental storage

2. Clear compartmented cases to hold all (and we do mean ALL) the different bead varieties

3. The cases fit the goods: 24-section cases for the smallest beads, 5-section cases for larger beads and chunky charms

THE "MOM, I NEED A PENCIL!" DRAWER

Just when we thought we had a single spot to ourselves—a home office devoted just to *our* needs—we remembered we are parents and there is no such thing. Sound familiar? You might as well make room for the supplies everyone in the house constantly asks for, and save yourself the time and energy of tracking them down.

1. Separate compartments for pens, highlighters, pencils, a pencil sharpener for when the pencils break, and mechanical pencils for those moments when everything else fails *because homework must still get done*

2. One small spot for your gift cards for those times when you need to treat yourself

3. Acrylic tape dispenser and stapler to match the transparent dividers

SMOKY STORAGE SHELVES

When our projects involve a married couple, we're usually brought in to focus on *her* items—but every now and then, we get to help out the husband, too. In this case, we were all too happy to organize the sleek black space and select storage options that complemented the cabinetry.

1. Document boxes for separating sentimental items from household documents to photos

2. Black-and-white books styled on either side of the black storage boxes to add a design element

3. Square storage—one to a shelf—for bulky accessories and travel items

4. Stackable clear drawers hold electronics, cords, and printer paper

TIP/ Create a docking station for your daily electronics (phone, laptop, etc.), so YOU can unplug from your devices while your DEVICES remain plugged in.

FAMILY PHOTOS

SPECIAL CARDS

RUBY

COCO

CRAFTS

CRAFTS

MAILING

ENVELOPES

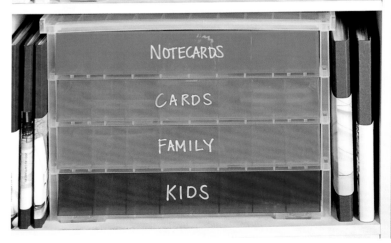

NOTECARDS

CARDS

FAMILY

KIDS

GIFT

OFFICE

OFFICE

OFFICE

APPLE

CABLES

CORD CONCEALERS

1

2

3

JOY CHO'S HOME OFFICE

We knew we had to bring an extra-colorful pop of rainbow into this office project for Joy Cho of the lifestyle brand Oh Joy! She is the queen of print and color, and a standard black-and-white aesthetic was not going to fly. So when we found this rainbow stacking drawer unit, we knew it was a winner.

1. Each child received her own sentimental storage box, while family memories and pictures were stored in photo boxes

2. Open bins and under-shelf organizers maximize shelf space

3. Crafts, cards, and supplies organized into a rainbow stackable drawer unit

TIP/ Most people don't have time to create photo albums anymore, so our Low-Bar Lifestyle firmly endorses photo storage boxes.

OFFICE ON A WALL

If you want your own space but don't have your own office, you can easily create one using an open wall. All it takes is an attached unit and a little bit of room. For this makeshift office, we took over a section of the guest bedroom. When the room isn't in use, it's a perfect getaway for working. When guests are expected, it can easily convert to a table that holds a pretty basket of towels and toiletries.

1. Wall unit includes a built-in desktop and extra shelving

2. Acrylic and gold office supplies displayed on a pegboard

3. Other (ahem, less pretty) office supplies stored in drawers to keep the desk clear

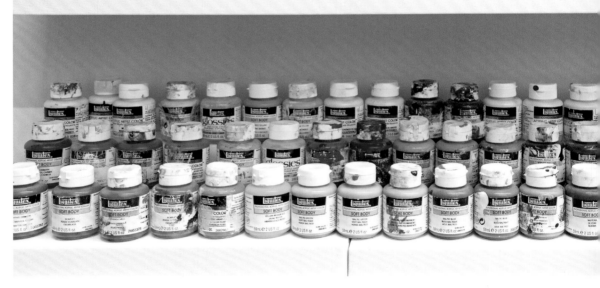

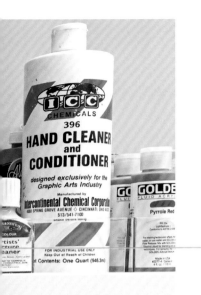

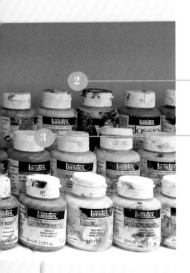

THE ART STUDIO

Sometimes an office isn't an office at all—it's a creative space where you get to have fun on a daily basis and also happen to earn a living. Sounds right up our alley! When we first walked into this artist's studio, our jaws dropped. ALL THE COLORS! We could hardly contain ourselves and got to create so many rainbows upon rainbows in lining up the various paints and pots of color.

1. Paintbrushes are stored in hair brush containers (hey, a brush is a brush . . .)

2. Paint bottles are propped up on three-tiered pantry shelves

3. Paint is lined up by type and shade for inspiration and convenience

TIP/ When shopping for products, think outside the box (literally!). Don't limit yourself by sticking to the "office section" when you might find even more useful supplies throughout the store. Walk down each aisle and get as many options as possible (you can always return what doesn't work). Just remember: **Clear eyes, full carts, can't lose.**

COMMAND STATION

If you have household paperwork, school schedules to keep track of, and never-ending bills, chances are you will need to file your documents and to-do lists. For the people who fall into this bucket, we like to create a home command station to hold all the incoming and outgoing paper.

1. Extra paperwork and finished projects filed into document boxes

2. Household projects and business documents stored in acrylic boxes of hanging file folders

3. Cards, stationery, and specialty paper kept on the desktop for easy note-writing

TIP/ Adding a pretty note-writing setup to your desk helps balance out the less pretty (and less fun) bill-paying setup!

HOME OFFICE

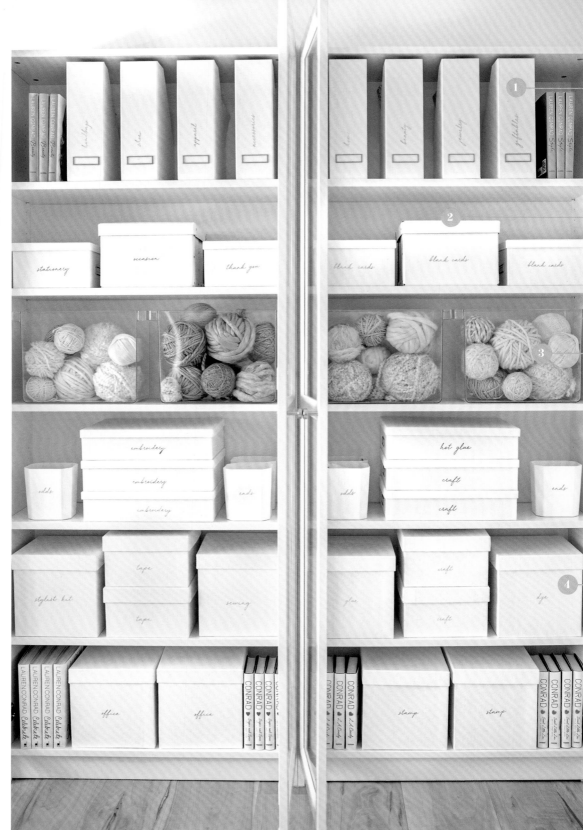

LAUREN CONRAD'S CRAFTING CLOSET

We have a handful of projects that will forever be on our "Absolute Most Favorite of All Time" list, and Lauren Conrad's office is at the top (it would be impossible to pick a single winner—that would be like picking children).

Lauren preferred concealed white storage for all her crafting/sewing/work supplies, but we knew we wanted to highlight her gorgeous knitting yarn, and she let us run with the idea of acrylic boxes. And so we all proceeded to sit on the floor happily making yarn balls like smitten kittens.

1. Magazines are organized by category and placed into proper holders

2. Thank-you cards and other stationery stored in photo boxes

3. Acrylic boxes show off beautiful balls of yarn sorted by color

4. White gift boxes are used as storage boxes and come from Lauren's fair trade shop, The Little Market

TIP/ Whenever possible, space out your containers to give them breathing room. The airiness and negative space help elevate the look.

THE
SUPPLY
CABINET

Not everyone has the space for an office closet, let alone an office. But scissors, supplies, and extra printer paper have to live somewhere. When you are short on space, remember to maximize your cabinets. You can turn any empty cabinet (even one in the kitchen!) into a supply station for your household.

1. Ongoing projects stored in top-shelf baskets

2. White and color paper stack in acrylic boxes

3. Brushes and scissors work perfectly in oversize cups

4. Compartmentalized caddies keep school and art supplies tidy

THE ARTS-AND-CRAFTS CLOSET

We have truly never met a tube of paint or set of markers that we didn't enjoy grouping into color-coordinated categories. And even though glitter is considered the herpes of the crafting world, as long as it doesn't permeate our *own* homes, we are very pleased to arrange it accordingly.

1. Bulky art and knitting supplies line the top and bottom shelves

2. Infrequently used party and gift supplies are stored in lidded lightweight bins

3. DIY and craft kits are kept in transparent bins to easily identify the items

4. Tall paint supplies, spray cans, and adhesives stored in jumbo bins to keep items upright

5. Smaller paint tubes work perfectly in divided stackable bins to maximize shelf space

PLAY SPACES

The first four spaces we covered were to help you slowly ramp up to the *next* four spaces, which are, admittedly, more challenging. But the process is the same—you're just applying it to more complicated rooms of the house. And while a playroom or kids' room tends to have significantly more to organize than an entryway closet, just remember that everything begins the same way: Take everything out, group things together, edit down, and assemble the categories back into an organized, labeled, and sustainable system.

But in case you need some additional pointers in this sticky (sometimes literally—kids tend to hoard half-eaten lollipops) space, here are some *extra* tips.

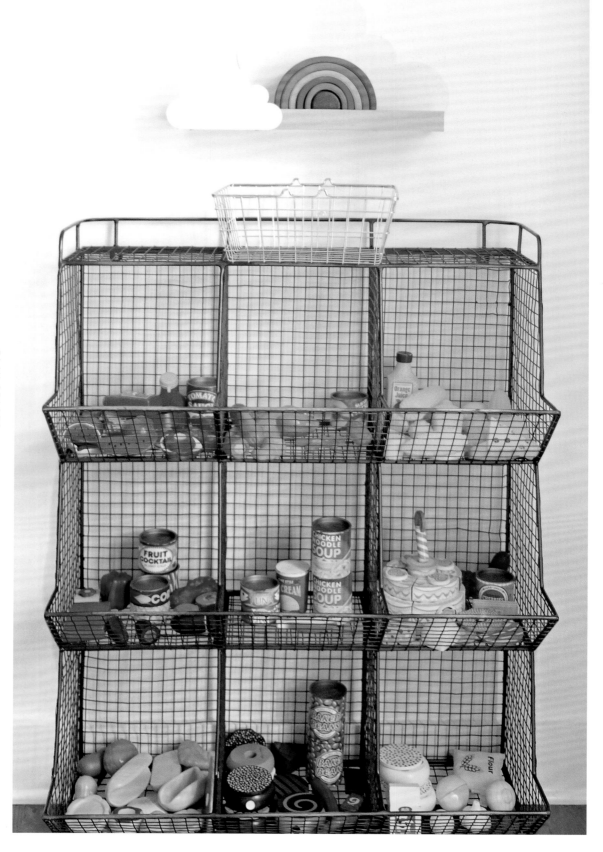

TOP 5 WAYS *to* MANEUVER THINGS AWAY FROM YOUR KIDS
(Who Already Have Too Much to Begin With)

1. **ALWAYS do the dirty work when they are out of the house.** The second they go to school, a playdate, or even once they fall asleep at night, run through your home with a donation bag like you're on *Supermarket Sweep,* and toss in anything that isn't nailed down. Or, if you're feeling generous, at *least* get rid of the items they haven't played with in months.

2. **NEVER ask your child, "Do you still like this?"** They will suddenly unearth a gravitational pull toward a stuffed animal they have probably never noticed before. Go with your gut and common sense, and purge the items you *know* they don't use.

3. **If something is missing parts, you will never find them.** Ever. Put an end to your misery by getting rid of the incomplete toy.

4. **If you wonder whether your kids will miss something once it's gone, move it into the garage or a storage closet for a couple of months.** We like to call this "purge purgatory," where things sit and wait while their fate is determined. On the rare occasion that your child asks for something you removed from the house, feign a touch of pensive thought, and say, "Hmm . . . I'll be on the lookout." Or you can always use the trusty "Oh, I put that in storage with your other art projects!" Someday they will realize that storage equals trash, but hopefully today is not that day.

5. Now, this one is really important, so listen carefully. **DO. NOT. KEEP. ANYTHING. FROM. A. PARTY. GIFT. BAG.** Those little trinkets get a twenty-hour-maximum shelf life in your house and then you take no prisoners and dispose of them immediately. We allow our kids to keep their favors only for the entire length of the car ride home from the party.

PLAY SPACES

SCHOOL SUPPLY DRAWER

Since we practice what we preach, let's start with the easiest space in a playroom: a drawer. In this particular case, it's a drawer full of crayons, pens, markers, and highlighters, because you never know when a school project is going to pop up and, as the Boy Scouts like to say, always be prepared.

1. Coloring essentials separated with in-drawer organizers

2. Crayons separated by color to help avoid the inevitable hunt for the ONE crayon they go looking for

3. Supplies lined up in ROYGBIV order to help inspire creativity and encourage the kids to put things back as neatly as they found them

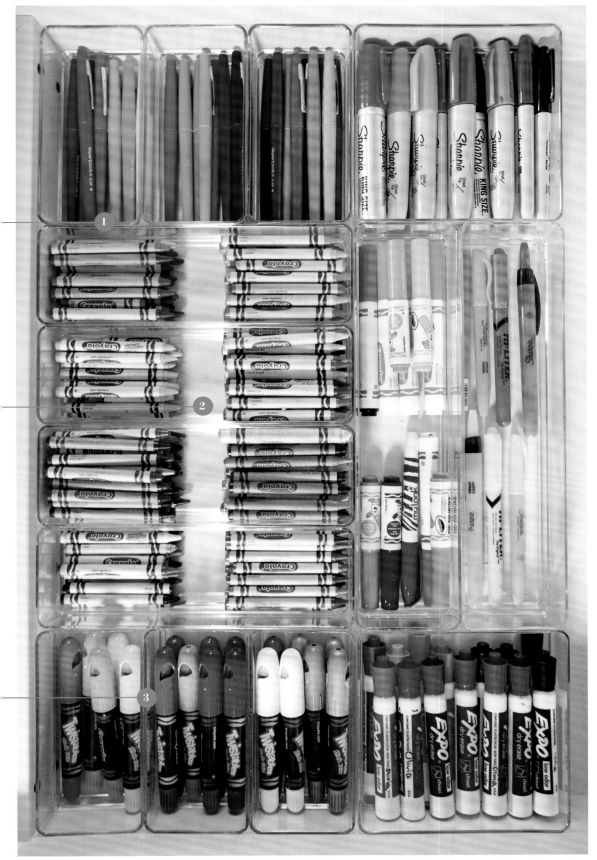

THE POSH PLAYROOM

We have never seen, and likely will never see, a playroom as incredible as this one, so we thought we could all drop our jaws together. Once we were able to collect ourselves (it took like five minutes of *OMG* and *I can't!* before we could get on with our work), we divided the room into zones: homework station, makerspace, reading corner, arts and crafts center, etc.

1. Books are lined up in rainbow order

2. Workbooks, school papers, and homework folders benefit from magazine holders

3. LEGOs are divided by color and type for easy building

4. Art turntable in the center of the table allows everyone to gather around

PLAY SPACES

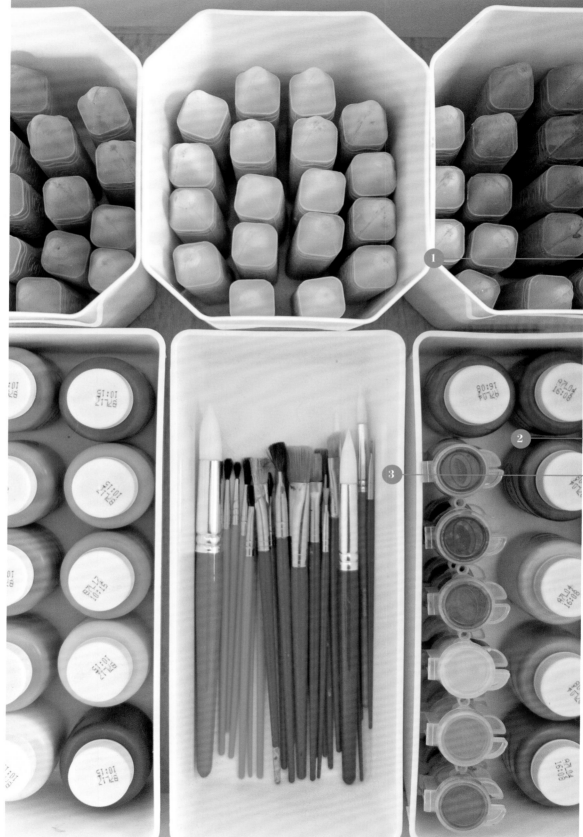

THE "GO PLAY OUTSIDE" DRAWER

We're always impressed when parents let their kids use messy art indoors (if our kids end up at these houses one day, they will probably be pretty annoyed), but sidewalk chalk is just not a thing that should ever be used in a house. It's right there in the name: "sidewalk." But playroom organization need not stay within the playroom. To encourage a clean home, we put together this drawer near the back door to make it easy to grab supplies on the way OUTSIDE.

1. Cups of sidewalk chalk make it easy for kids to grab without needing assistance

2. Rectangular cups to hold all the paint supplies

3. Plastic containers can be washed or wiped down when needed

EASY-ACCESS
TOY CLOSET

We have one core principle when organizing a space meant for kids: It has to be *easy*. Easy for them to access by themselves, easy for them to put things away, and easy for adults to assist, because—let's face it—duty will call. One of the ways we make it accessible is to use clear stacking storage with labels. The bins are lightweight and even suitable for little hands, and we provide all the visual cues necessary to assist in cleanup.

1. Blocks, cars, trains, and LEGO sets organized into stackable shoe boxes in two sizes appropriate for the contents

2. Toy cars separated by color for easy identification (i.e., to avoid the need to dump out all the bins to find the car they're looking for)

3. Flashcard cups to make homework a little bit more fun and enjoyable

TIP/ An organized play space turns cleanup into a game! Let your kids sort toys by color, create groupings, and stack categorized bins. It's a win for everyone!

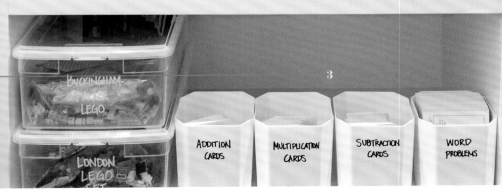

AMERICAN GIRL OBSESSED

If your child is suffering from the common syndrome of American Girl mania, know that we are here to help. We've tested multiple solutions to house the 12 million tiny bits and pieces, but in 99 percent of cases, the stacking shoe box helped to eliminate signs of frustration while preserving the euphoric joy of playing with miniature accessories.

1. Extra closet shelf used to hold the never-ending categories of clothing, tiny tutus, dance and gymnastic uniforms, and even extra hangers, because you never know when your child's doll will need an impromptu shopping trip

2. Labeled lightweight stacking shoe boxes make cleanup quick and easy

3. Tote hangers to hold actual human-size bags and not just the itty-bitty ones in bins

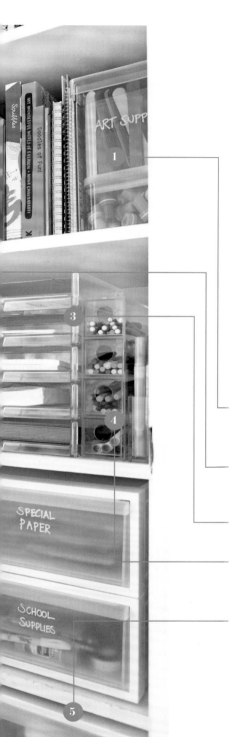

DEEP CRAFT CLOSET

To this day, this craft closet is one of our proudest organizing achievements. It might not look like a tough space, but it was packed. You would not believe what the living room looked like once this closet was unloaded onto the floor. There were piles of paint, glue, stickers, tape, coloring books, crafting paper, and DIY kits. Once the closet was cleared out, we realized that this seemingly small closet was, in fact, extra deep. Which can be problematic to maximize if you don't have the right supplies. Good thing we chose wisely, because two years later, it still looks this good! We've checked!

1. Acrylic file bins hold paint supplies and craft sets

2. An over-the-door organizer from Elfa created extra storage space

3. Letter trays used for papers and projects

4. Stacking acrylic storage drawers for pens, pencils, and markers

5. Stacking deep drawers helped us take advantage of the floor space

THE STUDY STATION

As kids get older, it gets more necessary to have a designated spot for doing homework. Whether that's part of the bedroom, the family room, or a playroom you transition into a study room, you might find endless options for getting the job done. One of our favorite ways to set up a working space is to install an Elfa wall unit with a desktop and open shelving. And of course we couldn't resist dressing it up with some rainbow accessories.

PLAY SPACES

1. Infrequently used coloring tools nicely displayed on the top shelf

2. Pegboard wall storage holds tools, supplies, and a ROYGBIV pop of colored pencils

3. Accessible jars of all the pens, pencils, and highlighters needed for homework

4. Desktop is large enough for two computers, and both monitors sit on risers for extra storage

TIP/ Find a fun, decorative object (like this glass-and-gold terrarium) to hold unexpected supplies like washi tape. It's a great way to uniquely showcase a collection of items.

THE
CRAFT CUP
DRAWER

It's kind of ironic how obsessed we are with crafting supplies, considering we've never actually used them to *craft*. We are highly organized yet incredibly uncrafty people. To be honest, the thought of a bunch of tiny buttons or googly eyes being carelessly strewn all over the playroom is rather unsettling. But to our clients who are brave enough to allow these tiny bits and pieces into their homes, we thank you, because we're thrilled to organize them. For *you*. Not *us*.

1. Small containers are an ideal fit for shallow drawers

2. Beads, bits, and buttons organized into their own cups

3. Larger crafting supplies and tools line the sides

TIP/ Instead of purchasing small craft cups, you can always use Dixie cups, cleaned yogurt containers, or even teacups for storage.

GWYNETH PALTROW'S PLAYROOM

We will never normalize the fact that we were in Gwyneth Paltrow's playroom because we continue to die over it every time we think about it, *as one should.* We get asked a lot about our favorite projects, and this playroom is definitely in The Home Edit Hall of Fame. Not just because it belongs to GP, but because we pulled out every tool in our proverbial kit to turn this room into a showstopper and let it live its best life.

1. Books and stuffed animals lined up in rainbow order are ready for downtime

2. Games, puzzles, LEGO sets, and science kits are on the opposite side for stimulating activity time

3. Drawers hold art supplies, activity books, and dolls

HANGING TOY SHELVES

If you don't have extra closets, drawers, and cabinets to dedicate to toys and crafts, an industrial hanging wall unit is the perfect answer. It can hang in a living room, bedroom, or playroom and has the added bonus of *actually* being nice to look at. The smokestack of the ship even makes a perfect cup for pens and pencils!

1. Colored acrylic cases help organize crayons and craft supplies while providing a functional and finished look

2. Industrial metal trays used as inserts to hold drawing paper and completed "doodles"

3. Stacking shoe boxes for blocks and building toys

TIP/ These wall-hanging units work perfectly in a nursery for holding diapers and wipes, then transition right to toys and books as your child grows.

UNDER-STAIR STORAGE

In the same way *The Wizard of Oz* gave everyone a healthy fear of tornadoes, Harry Potter didn't exactly provide positive press on closets under the stairs. So we want to firmly endorse using them to store all things *except* children. You definitely don't want to do that. But you *can* use them to store things your children *own*—and isn't that a better idea?

1. Extra-deep drawers and bins store craft and sewing supplies

2. Open bins keep cups of pens, pencils, markers, and stickers handy

3. Large stacking drawers hold gift and party supplies

CLOSETS

Tackling a closet is not for the faint of heart. It's essentially an organizing project scattered with emotional land mines and decision-making trip wires. Just when you think you might be making progress, you'll come across a dress that reminds you of an event you went to, or a sweater you wore almost every day that you were pregnant with your firstborn. And even if you make it through those hurdles, you may eventually find clothing that forces you to confront the size you were ten years ago. But if you create some goals and ground rules (see also "Rules for Getting Rid of Stuff," page 41), you can make it through to the other side relatively unscathed.

CLOSET CODE OF CONDUCT

1. **The first rule of your cleaning your closet is to not talk about cleaning your closet.** Not with your friends, who want to get their mitts on your giveaways; not with your mother-in-law, who will do a spot check to make sure all the scarves and sweaters she gave you are still in there; and not with your daughter, who all of a sudden will plead with you to keep some vintage something for her that she will never ever have any interest in. And if you're married, you DEFINITELY do not want to talk about it with your spouse, since he or she will likely check on your progress and annoy you endlessly.

2. **Be realistic.** We cannot stress this enough. If you find a tiny pair of low-rise denim from your pre-pregnancy days, just say goodbye.

3. **Go with your gut.** If for *whatever* reason you don't really like something in your closet, you probably will not *grow* to like it in the coming months. And you don't want clothing you don't like taking up valuable real estate.

4. **Get rid of the guilt**—whether someone gave it to you or you spent a lot of money on something and feel bad getting rid of it. DO NOT FEEL BAD. You should feel bad that it's taking up valuable real estate in your closet instead of something you actually like! Instead, you can sell it online or in a store if it might have value, you can give it away to someone who might like it, or you can donate it to someone who might need it. All are good options, and none of them includes holding on to something unnecessary.

5. **No backsies.** Once you decide to get rid of an item, it cannot make its way back into your closet. That is a slippery slope. Stay strong, and keep the donation pile sacred.

RACHEL ZOE'S CLOSET

Establishing order in Rachel Zoe's enormous closet is somewhat like competing in an organizing Olympics. We've actually discussed what would happen in such a competition, and we feel like we would totally CRUSH IT, but that's neither here nor there. For the moment, RZ's closet will have to be the closest we come to such a reality.

1. Extra-large bags and duffels line the top

2. Jackets hung by designer, color, and type

3. Delicate jackets wrapped for extra protection

4. Each stall divider labeled

TIP/ Fitting this many jackets requires the help of a high-quality slim hanger. It's an initial splurge, but the investment is worthwhile!

NO DRESSER, NO PROBLEM

Lining up baskets on a shelf essentially creates a makeshift dresser. We created this one in a bathroom linen closet, but you can use any available closet shelf. Line them on the top shelf or underneath hanging items, or repurpose shoe cubbies—every inch of space is fair game!

1. His-and-hers baskets ("his" on the higher shelves and "hers" on the lower shelves) hold foldables, while hanging clothes remain in the closet

2. Shirts file-folded to maximize the basket and make them easy to identify

3. In-drawer dividers placed directly in the basket to keep socks organized

4. Stool placed at the bottom to make the top shelf easy to reach

TIP/ If you've already read Marie Kondo's *The Life-Changing Magic of Tidying Up,* then you know about the magic of file folding. If not, it's a folding method that turns stacks of clothing upright so you can see everything you have. You will never have to turn your drawer (or basket!) inside out looking for a shirt.

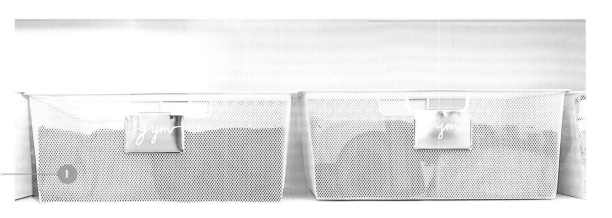

THE
SHOE
CLOSET

Interior designer Julie Couch really knew what she
was doing when she put this shoe wall in her master
closet. She made sure each shelf was high enough
to accommodate her highest heels, and she also
made sure there was boot storage for her highest-
heeled boots. A smart layout always makes our
job easier (even if it means we waste a little time
*ooh*ing and *ahh*ing).

1. Tallest boots placed in cubbies with a boot clip
to hold them together

2. Heels and flats displayed on open shelving

3. Sandals, running shoes, and winter boots go in
labeled shoe boxes on shelves and the floor

TIP/ If you don't have built-in boot
storage, adjust your closet shelves
to accommodate tall boots, or use an adjustable
bookshelf for shoe storage. If the shelf fits, use it!

THE SCHOOL AND SPORTS CLOSET

Kids don't just go to school anymore; they have about six hundred other clubs, sports, and teams that fill every remaining minute of the day. So when we are organizing for school-age kids, we try to account for each extracurricular activity (within reason!) to make the transition from uniform to uniform a bit easier.

1. Over-the-door unit to hold uniforms for basketball, tennis, and volleyball

2. Acrylic drawers on shelving to keep swimsuits and loungewear together

3. Clothes hung on nonslip hangers to avoid them from falling off

4. Tote hangers hold backpacks upright

5. Stacking acrylic shoe holders take advantage of the floor space

THOMAS RHETT
AKINS'S CLOSET

For anyone who thinks women always own more
clothing than men, let us be the first to tell you that
is not always the case. Sometimes they own way,
way, WAY more . . . But in all fairness, country music
singer Thomas Rhett is known for his great style, and
we wanted to figure out a way to store everything
appropriately while showcasing his favorite items.

1. Special-occasion boots and dress shoes
stored in shoe boxes on the top shelf

2. Running shoes (the clear favorite!) are displayed
on the shoe wall

3. Casual shoes stored in shoe boxes in the
center column

4. Hats are stored in pull-out drawers to keep
them free from dust

5. Shirts, sweatshirts, and jackets hung separately

TIP/ When tight on space, don't forget to
look up! There's usually additional
storage options at the top of a closet, and it's a
perfect spot for bulky luggage or seasonal items.

BARE-BONES CLOSET

Some closets come with nothing but a hanging rod and, if we're *lucky,* maybe a shelf. So we try to come up with some creative solutions to maximize the space. By now you've caught on to our penchant for over-the-door storage. It's just so *helpful* that we encourage everyone to feel as passionately about door units as we do. And don't get us started on our love of carts. Who wouldn't want one?

1. Baskets for travel and linens line the top

2. Hook added for hats

3. Closet doors used for running shoes and sandal storage

4. Rolling cart can easily be moved out of the way

THE BALLROOM CLOSET

You could honestly hold a high school cotillion class in this closet. You could probably even hold a small wedding ceremony and reception in this closet. In fact, the term *closet* might not really apply here. Nevertheless, when we set out to organize it (honestly, it was pretty well organized already), we wanted to go the extra mile to make it even *more* picture perfect.

1. Activewear tops and bottoms in first stall on the left

2. Shirts, sweaters, jackets, dresses, and pants hung in separate stalls

3. Accessories, winter items, and undergarments put away in drawers and cabinets

(continues)

4. Tennis and workout clothes hung according to color and type

5. Athletic shoes stored on the floor while dressy shoes are displayed on shelves

6. Earrings and necklaces displayed in acrylic organizers

7. Watches stored in stacking acrylic cases

8. Bracelets placed on velvet holders to keep them from scratching

CLOSETS

SMALL SPACE CLOSET

Do you have any idea how much we wanted to add an over-the-door unit to this closet? Yes, you probably do . . . And it was downright painful that the rod didn't fit on these charming original doors. But when other options fail, hooks will never let you down! We were able to hang the handbags, and take advantage of the floor space by creating a "chest of floor drawers."

1. Lesser-used sandals and heels go on the upper shelf

2. Handbags hung on a door hook

3. Denim folded into modular drawers

4. Most-used sneakers and boots stacked in floor shoe boxes

TIP/ Stacking shoe boxes on the floor helps optimize vertical space and keeps your shoes dust-free!

CLOSETS

HIS SIDE
OF THE CLOSET

Every now and again we get to organize the husband's side of the closet. It's usually the bottom of the priority list, but sometimes we get to spend a few minutes sprucing it up. This closet was definitely a Nashville-specific project, since we had to account for multiple cowboy hats!

1. Hats lined up on the top shelf

2. Shoes organized in order from dressiest to most casual on a tilted shelf for easy identification

3. Wooden shoe inserts

4. Sandals put away in shoe boxes

TIP/ Since sandals are less bulky than other shoes, you can typically store more than one pair in each shoe box.

THE ADULTS-HAVE-ACTIVITIES-TOO CLOSET

Kids aren't the only ones who play tennis and go swimming! And for those lucky enough to have hobbies (we personally don't have hobbies outside of eating and sometimes sleeping), we are more than happy to create a dedicated space in the closet for everyone's swimsuits, yoga clothes, and tennis skirts.

1. Cold-weather activewear stored on top shelf

2. Tote bags suspended from hooks on the upper rack

3. Swimsuits and cover-ups folded in lined baskets to protect the delicate material

4. Tennis skirts and jackets neatly hung with hangers evenly spaced

KACEY MUSGRAVES'S CLOSET

When Kacey Musgraves started building out her new closet she asked us to help with the layout. We're often called in *after* a closet is built, so to be able to choose the shelving and the placement of the hanging rods, and even install a special accessories station, made the project extra special. Not to mention the fact that we were able to organize rainbow-fringe handbags, cactus high heels, and his-and-hers cowboy boots.

1. Handbags hung on tote hangers

2. Sunglasses, jewelry, and accessories in stacked clear lidded cases

3. Painting of Elvis crying placed by Kacey at the last minute!

4. Special shoes and handbags on display

5. Long necklaces on a gold horseshoe hook

6. Seasonal clothes and extra hats in upper baskets

7. Her clothes on the right, his clothes on the left

KITCHEN

This room is such a massively important part of a home that we decided to break it up into two chapters: one for the kitchen and another dedicated to the pantry. (Kind of like how the seventh Harry Potter movie needed to be split into two films. Some things just need more room to breathe.)

Kitchens tend to be stumbling blocks for a lot of people, so before embarking on the entire thing at once, try to section it off into zones. You can even give yourself a road map by making cheat-sheet sticky notes to mark off each cabinet and drawer. As with every first project, we suggest starting with a drawer—it can be a utensil drawer, kitchen tools drawer, or even the junk drawer. Pick your poison, and dive in.

THE JUNK-NO-MORE DRAWER

You never know when you'll need a battery or a rubber band, or have to sign a card before you run out the door. The key difference between an *organized* junk drawer and one that makes you shout, "DON'T OPEN THAT!" when guests come over is a thoughtful edit and lots of containment. One hundred percent of junk drawers have *actual* junk in them that can be thrown out—everything left just needs a home.

1. Unpacked batteries are *always* stored separately for safety

2. Cords, change, and clips get their own mini container

3. Bulky flashlights and tools placed on the sides to hold the organizers in place

THE PAPER-LINED DRAWER

Of all the kitchen drawers we've organized, this remains our favorite. These drawers belong to our DIY mentor Elsie Larson from A Beautiful Mess, and when organizing for the queen, you pull out all the stops. Her kitchen is full of mint greens and pale blush tones, so we thought a large sheet of ombré paper would make an excellent drawer liner.

1. Everyday utensils and cutlery in the front portion of the drawer

2. Entertaining items in the back portion—except for the gold alligator cheese knives, since those needed to be front and center

3. Expandable utensil trays mixed with modular sizes to get a perfect fit

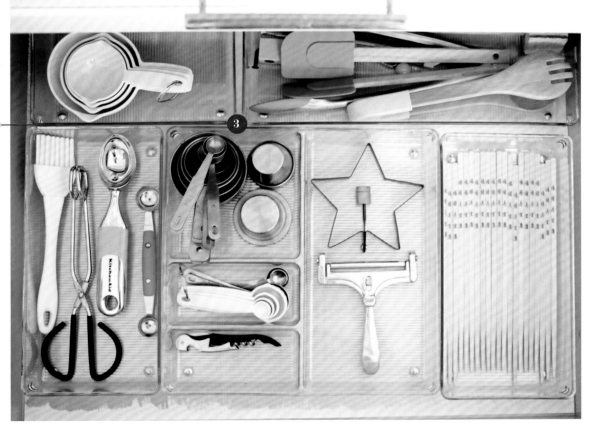

hello love
RISE and SHINE
girls JUST WANNA HAVE coffee
CUTCO
1
2
3

THE COFFEE
STATION

Whenever we organize a kitchen, we try to sneak in
a beverage station. Whether it's a coffee cabinet, a
tea caddy, or a smoothie station, it's just fun to leave
behind something special. We admit that sometimes
we get carried away just to find out that our client gave
up caffeine six months ago or really can't stand tea . . .
but MOST of the time, it's a real crowd-pleaser.

1. Coffee cups organized directly above the coffee
maker for quick access

2. Coffee pods in clear jars so choosing flavors is easy

3. Tray assembled with coffee and tea serving
accessories

EVERYTHING UNDER THE KITCHEN SINK

We take pride in all our work, but there's something very satisfying about transforming the cabinet underneath the kitchen sink. When someone mentally prepares to organize their *own* sink cabinet, they seem to be somewhere on the spectrum of totally vexed to completely grossed out. Because we believe everything should be multipurpose, here is the win-win way to clean out your cabinet:

1. Extra cleaning supplies line the back for restocking the caddies as needed

2. Bin contains back stock of hand soaps

3. Cleaning caddy and sponge caddy in turntables for easy access

4. Easy-to-clean containers—because, yes, even cleaning containers need to be wiped down

SINK CABINET CARDIO

1. Squat down.

2. Take out anything gross, leaking, sticky, or old.

3. Rise to a standing position.

4. Turn and throw it all in the trash.

5. Repeat.

See? Easy. And for everything else—just contain and label it.

ENTERTAINING CABINET

Our maximum number of dinner guests is certainly in the single digits—and we each own party banners that say "PLEASE LEAVE BY 7." So I wouldn't take our word on entertaining etiquette, but we can certainly help you organize all the components. And if you want to open up your home to a bunch of people who will probably fail to use all the coasters you strategically place in each room, well, that's your call.

1. Outdoor supplies organized in waterproof plastic bins to keep outside while entertaining

2. Outdoor plates, cups, straws, and napkins on the top shelf

3. Cutlery stored in individual plastic cups to keep categories separated

4. Linens, placemats, and napkin rings on the bottom shelf

THE HEALTHY FRIDGE AND FREEZER

It turns out, if you eat only fruits and veggies, your fridge and freezer will look as good as you do. It gives a whole new meaning to the term "eat the rainbow," and we are very much on board! On board for *others*. We don't eat this way.

1. Milk, water, and juice line the top in glass pitchers and acrylic holders

2. Precut fruit in glass food storage containers

3. Meal-prep and produce in open containers and drawers

4. Frozen fruit in separate bins for easy snacking (EVEN THEIR FROZEN TREATS ARE HEALTHY . . . HOW?!)

KIDS' DISHES DRAWER

We get asked a lot about what to do with kids' items in a kitchen. They always seem to be in unruly piles and make the inside of a cabinet look like a colorful bomb went off. There are a few ways to make the dishes and sippy cups work, but one of our go-to methods is using a drawer. And you have the added bonus that kids are able to help themselves.

1. Dishes and snack cups lined up in bins rather than stacked

2. Bottle parts in separate compartments

3. Utensils organized into cups

4. Sippy cups lined up into rows

TIP/ Edit out your kids' plastic dishes on a regular basis. Because if Elsa's face is peeling off the dinner plate, it's time to . . . let it go. Sorry, could not resist.

THE NURSING DRAWER

The only things more vexing than kids' dishes and snack cups are bottle parts. Certain bottles seem to have a minimum of seven hundred parts, and they all need to be individually cleaned, sterilized, and dried. Eight times a day. Such is life with a baby. The good news, however, is that if you create a designated zone for all the supplies, you can keep a tiny shred of your sleepless sanity. It's a very small shred, but it's SOMETHING.

1. Pumping parts and milk storage bottles organized next to each other

2. Feeding bottles and extra nipples in their own bin

3. Sterilizer, food storage containers, and nursing pads line the sides

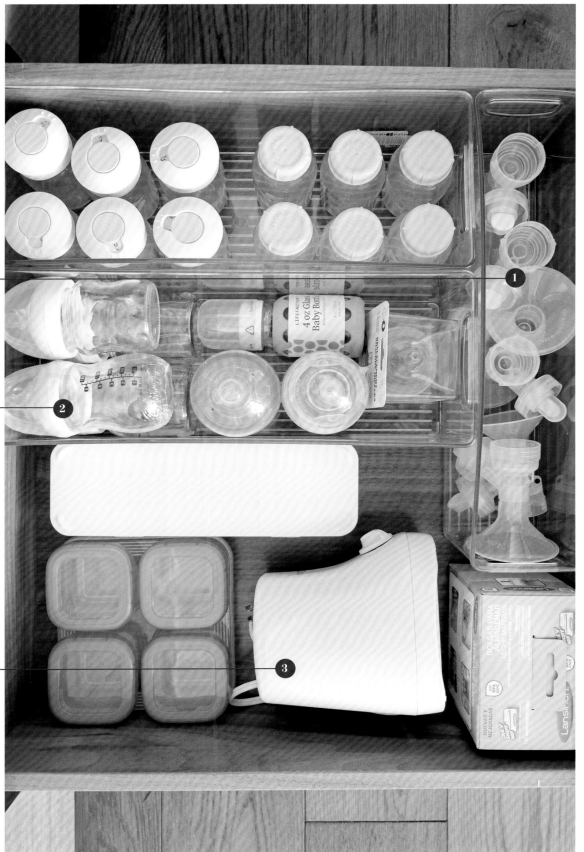

GLASS-FRONT CABINETS

A cabinet with glass shelves might as well not even have doors. You have to commit to keeping it relatively perfect because there is nothing for things to hide behind. Normally, we use glass cabinets for decorative dishes or barware, but sometimes you need all the cabinet space you can get and can't sacrifice prime shelving for china you never use. The answer: coordinated canisters.

1. Rarely used entertaining platters and bowls at the very top

2. Canisters of rice, pasta, and dry goods on the second shelf

3. Canisters of baking sugars and flours on the shelf closest to the stand mixer

TIP/ Even if you don't have glass-front cabinets, losing product packaging for canisters makes any cabinet look infinitely better!

GLASS-FRONT FRIDGE

Perhaps more stressful than a glass-front cabinet would be a see-through fridge. You can't get away with making it look nice by displaying a single decorative plate or canister collection, and a fridge has a higher rotation of contents than even a pantry. Just know that if you opt for a glass fridge, it's kind of like getting a cat . . . you're going to have to take care of it at *least* a few times a week.

1. Milk, juice, and eggs transferred to pitchers and egg trays to reduce the amount of visible packaging

2. Bins keep condiments, spreads, and sauces contained

3. Prepared foods and precut fruit transferred to glass food storage containers

4. Opaque drawers utilized for dairy and protein

TIP/ Use a washable window marker to label expiration dates on milk or egg containers.

PANTRY

Our tombstones will likely read, "Pantry perfectionists who were canister enthusiasts, turntable advocates, and women entirely committed to labeling all things." We just really, really, *really* love pantries. There is truly NO space we love to organize more, and we will take them in all shapes and sizes. We're going to show you some of our greatest hits, some tricky near misses (we REFUSED to let an awkward corner be our Waterloo!), and some really simple setups you can easily replicate in your own home.

Before you embark on organizing your own pantry, just know that it is generally the toughest spot in the house . . . and once you empty the shelves and see that you're surrounded by a sea of pasta boxes and cereal and canned goods, you might panic. We have panicked. Many times. You look at everything around you and think, "HOW ON EARTH DID *ALL THIS* COME OUT OF *THERE*?!" Usually, the reason is because everything was stacked on top of everything else and shoved on the shelves. That often means the shelves *were* being maximized—just in a horribly disorganized way. And the job at hand, should you choose to accept it, is to untangle the web and put everything back in a systemized and contained way.

This is where your THE training is going to come into play, because with a pantry, you need to be disciplined with your steps. Do not get distracted by shiny objects, because unless you plan on just throwing everything away and starting over, once you empty out the pantry, you need to find a way to put it all back in. So let's have one more refresh before taking the final exam:

1. **Measure your space** so you can pick supplies that will take advantage of every inch.

2. **Take everything out** and group it into piles as you go (such as breakfast, dinner, and snacks).

3. **Go through each pile** and toss anything that's expired, overly duplicative, leaking, etc.

4. **Organize the remaining piles** into the containers you purchased.

5. **Systematically arrange the groupings** in your space so that it makes sense for your household.

THE CABINET PANTRY

Some of you are probably like, *Okay, thanks for nothing—I don't even* have *a pantry*. But you *do* have to keep your food somewhere. Even a granola bar needs a place to live! And cabinets make great places for food storage, as long as you still create systems in the small space.

1. Tea caddy directly above beverages

2. Breakfast, dinner, baking, and beverage categories separated into their own cabinet-size bins

3. Spices, sauces, and condiments on turntables to help reach the items on the higher shelf

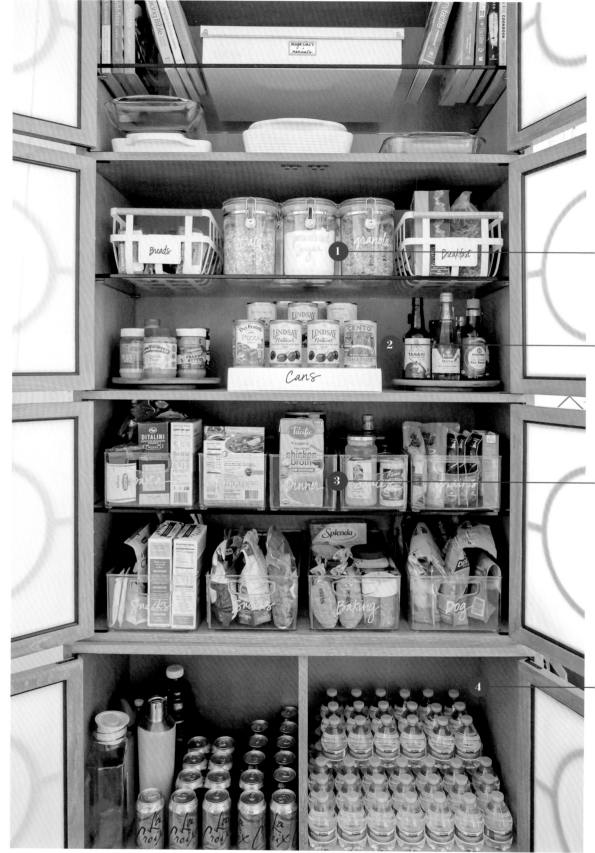

FREESTANDING
FOOD STORAGE

If you have an extra-small kitchen and can't devote any cabinet to a makeshift pantry, you can always add a freestanding one to any nearby wall. With the doors closed, it's just a nice piece of furniture, and when the doors open, they reveal a pretty perfect pantry (if we do say so ourselves).

1. Breakfast and baking in see-through storage to keep contents visible

2. Spreads, cans, and condiments on risers and turntables

3. Food groupings in extra-deep bins that can pull out like drawers

4. Beverages on the bottom shelf to support the extra weight of the higher shelves

---

PANTRY PROWESS

In the event that you experience pantry paralysis, here are words of wisdom:

1. Not all expiration dates are created equal. If your chips are expired, it probably just means they are stale and you can decide whether to toss them. However, if something perishable has expired (oils, nuts, broth, etc.), it must go. Period. Canned goods *can* go bad, so be sure to check your back stock.

2. Remove as much packaging as possible so things fit more easily in bins and canisters.

3. Keep only the amount of food on hand that your pantry can realistically hold. We aren't all meant to shop at Costco, so consider your space constraints and stock up accordingly.

THE
CHEF'S
PANTRY

Normally, we would never recommend putting
EVERYTHING in a jar or canister. That would take a lot
of work to maintain, since you would have to refill
the jars after every trip to the store *and* let the jars
run almost empty before restocking. We are not
accustomed to living on the edge, but in this instance,
our client is a chef—and since she felt confident
about this plan, we felt good about it, too. Also, it was
REALLY PRETTY to look at, so we got on board quickly.

1. Dry goods and snacks in a variety of jars and on
risers for maximum visibility

2. Most-used flours and sugar on the worktop

3. Produce in stackable, breathable baskets to hold
different types

1

Soba Noodles · Whole Wheat Penne · elbow macaroni · Quinoa · White Beans · split peas · Rice · Panko · Couscous

dry goods

Wasabi Soy Sauce Triscuits · Triscuits · cashews · raisins · pistachios · Walnut Pieces · Roasted almonds · pecans · Mixed Nuts

Snacks

2

Bread Flour

3

THE
MORNING
ROUTINE

Remember when we said we liked creating beverage stations in the kitchen? We like creating them in pantries, too. Pretty much anywhere remotely within reason receives a beverage setup. And when we saw how much tea lived in this pantry, we practically fell over ourselves lining everything up in perfect colorful rows.

1. Cereals, oatmeal, and pancake mix transferred to glass canisters with scoops

2. Tea boxes lined up on pull-out pantry drawers

3. ROYGBIV organization for the tea boxes—for purely no reason other than it would have been a missed opportunity. (We typically use the rainbow in a way that's applicable to organization, but not this time. Girls can have their fun, okay?)

TIP/ If the product packaging is both functional and attractive, like these tea boxes, feel free to store them as is! No additional products or supplies required.

BUILD-YOUR-OWN PANTRY

Even if you don't have an entire room to devote to a pantry, you can make a DIY version using the same wall units we showed you previously (see page 219). This particular pantry was installed in a space just off the kitchen, and now it qualifies as a pantry dream—and an attainable one, at that.

1. Back stock baskets on the upper shelves

2. Pasta, grains, and cereal transferred to canisters lining the side shelves

3. Canned goods and condiments line the center and side shelves, with the most frequently used ones stored in the center

4. Stand mixer stored on the worktop with the rest of the space kept clear

5. Snacks and beverages divided in pull-out drawers

BLACK-AND-WHITE PANTRY

It's well established that we are both pantry proponents and black-and-white believers, so this pantry gets a teacher's pet award. Plus, it was fun to work with some different materials and play with grayscale instead of the rainbow!

1. Cereals, baking flours, and protein powders lined up in narrow canisters

2. Large groupings in concealed wooden crates keep everything monotone

3. Striking black labels make finding what you need even easier

4. Bakeware down low; blenders and entertaining supplies up high

TIP/ Consider which items are heaviest, and keep them at a more accessible height, even if you use them infrequently. You don't want to lift heavy or awkward items over your head.

PARK AVENUE PANTRY

Some of the most beautiful homes in America do *not* have walk-in pantries. You can achieve the same level of functionality and quality of aesthetic in a pullout pantry as you can in a walk-in, but you need to be mindful of your products and which shelves they go on. For this pantry, we tried to make everything as visible as possible, and we used the pull-out drawers wisely.

1. Sweet snacks and weekend cereal on the upper shelves, out of reach

2. Dried fruit, nuts, and smoothie supplies in stacking canisters

3. Cereal canisters line the front of the drawer, breakfast items in the back bins

4. Kids' healthy snacks in the bottom two drawers

1
2
3
4
6
EVERYTHING I WANT TO EAT
PLENTY
GJELINA
ORGANIC VIRGIN COCONUT OIL
SMEG
THE MOUNTAIN VALLEY

MANDY MOORE'S PANTRY

"Mandy Moore" rhymes with "store," and that's the kind of pantry she was looking for. (Is that the first ever pantry nursery rhyme?) If you have followed along as Mandy has beautifully remodeled her current home, you know it is designed to actual perfection. So of course her pantry had to live up to its surroundings!

1. Bulk back stock on the top shelves

2. Food is kept out of reach of the dogs

3. Custom spice jars organized on turntables

4. Appliances kept on the worktop to keep the kitchen counters clean

5. Food groupings on side shelves (not pictured, but we promise there *is* food!)

6. Paper towels and water bottles unpacked and beautifully lined up on the bottom shelves

NO-PANTRY SOLUTION, PART ONE

We always tell you to start with a drawer, but sometimes you can *end* with a drawer, too. If you don't have a pantry and you run out of cabinet space, move on to the drawers! They can be the perfect spot to set up a snack station, beverage supplies, or a spice solution.

1. Spices transferred from disparate containers to uniform jars to achieve a perfect fit AND create a customized aesthetic

2. Spice jars lined up in alphabetical order for quick identification

3. Grab-and-go protein bars and tea supplies unpacked and placed in separate compartments

TIP/ You can line up spice jars by alphabet, color, or size. It's your personal preference, so choose whichever system you can best maintain!

NO-PANTRY SOLUTION, PART TWO

With the help of drawer organizers, we were able to fit breakfast, snacks, and kids' items in a single space—no pantry required.

1. Snack bars, fruit pouches, and nuts in the back horizontal sections

2. Breakfast bars and oatmeal in the front vertical sections

3. Items lying flat rather than standing to accommodate drawer height

THE SPEAKING-OF-SNACKS PANTRY

When it comes to snacks, this pantry takes the proverbial cake, all puns intended. Yes, we also crushed the canister situation, but we will get to that in a minute. Can we just pause to lovingly look at all the snacks in perfect rainbow order and not focus on the fact that nothing is organic and packaging causes waste? We're here to organize the pantry, not instruct people how to eat!

1. Crackers and chips in canisters and packaged grab-and-go items in divided open bins

2. Cereal, flours, grains, and dried fruit and nuts transferred to canisters to keep items fresher longer

3. ROYGBIV snack setup creates a fun way for kids to help themselves and encourages them to keep it neat

4. Produce stored in baskets on the bottom shelf

TIP/ When you transfer grains that have specific cook times, you can label the back of the canister with instructions, or cut out the back and slip it inside.

WIRE
SHELVING
PANTRY

By far, the most feared type of food storage is the wire shelving pantry. It's one thing to organize pantry shelves, but when those shelves have gaping holes, it just feels like a trap. But fear not, because there are some helpful tricks of the trade that will remove the wire shelving stumbling block.

1. Bins on the top shelf are shallower and have an extended handle to make the snacks easier to access

2. Dinner, breakfast, and snack items organized into bins with flat bases that will not get caught on the shelves

3. Cereal transferred into canisters with square bases, since skinny cereal boxes are unstable on the wire slats

TIP/ When possible, have a heavy-duty clear plastic shelf liner cut to fit your wire shelf's dimensions, or buy a precut one at a hardware store.

GWYNETH PALTROW'S PANTRY

It's one thing to have the honor of organizing Gwyneth Paltrow's pantry, but when GP herself told us we were going to be in *goop,* we screamed audibly and loudly— there was also some jumping involved. And we would do it all over again, because there is no other appropriate reaction; all decorum can be put on hold. With that in mind, we close the Pantry chapter with the crown jewel of all pantries.

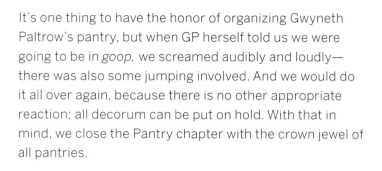

1. Up top, back stock bins for restocking shelves are at the ready

2. Canned goods in clear stacking bins take advantage of the height of the shelves

3. Bulk dinner, breakfast, and snack items in oversize bins

4. Condiments and spreads, organized and labeled by type (breakfast, sweet, international cuisines, etc.), line the pantry doors

5. Most frequently used nuts, dried fruit, and grains stored in hermetically sealed jars to maintain freshness

6. School snacks separate into their own bins for easy lunch packing

TIP/ Stick a piece of dry-erase tape to the back or bottom of a reusable jar so you can write down expiration dates.

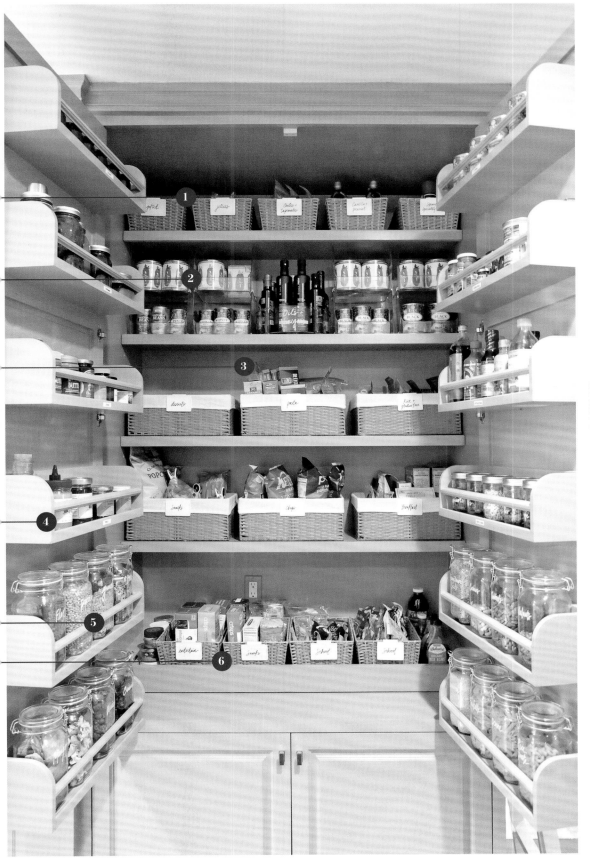

the upkeep

(AKA WE PROMISE IT WILL STAY LIKE THIS)

We're not going to lie to you: Keeping your newly organized space looking beautiful will take effort. It won't be difficult, and it won't be painful, but it will require a commitment to the order you just created. It's like any other kind of maintenance, whether it's your home, your car, or your health—it takes some vigilance, some part of your brain to track what needs to be regularly checked in order to keep things in good working order. The good news is that by going through the purging, editing, and organizing steps we've outlined earlier in this book, you've innately created a system that's essentially plug and play. If you've done it right, you should have a system that works not only for the size of your space and the amount of your things, but also the function of that particular space. So with a little effort—we're talking keeping-a-houseplant-alive effort (a succulent, not an orchid)—you can easily maintain it.

Luckily, the very essence of the THE process is rigged so that your spaces will be as easy as possible to keep up. Every single thing we ask you to do is for a reason, and it's not only so your closet/pantry/fridge will look good on Instagram. From paring down to labeling to color coordination—and making a space just as beautiful as it is functional—there's a method to the madness. Now let's quickly discuss how to avoid a complete do-over in six months.

TIPS *for* LONG-TERM SUCCESS

ENLISTING OTHER PEOPLE TO HELP

Something we hear all the time is "My roommates will never maintain this" or "My kids are going to rip this apart." But don't assume that just because you live with other people, maintaining an organized space will be impossible. As we said before, it will be *some* work, but not much. Think of it this way: Do you use a utensil sorter in your silverware drawer? If so, doesn't everyone automatically agree that the spoons all go in one section, forks in another, and knives in another?

Following an organized system in any space is no different! It's as easy as unloading your dishwasher and putting your silverware away, especially if you followed our advice about labeling and using the ROYGBIV system (see pages 47 and 49). There is not a partner too oblivious or roommate so inconsiderate that they can't participate. And while we're at it, we also don't think there's a child too young to start joining in on the organization action. We have personally turned our children into organizing apprentices, so we fully encourage you to enlist your children as well. In fact, it is mission critical to your long-term results that *everyone* in your household get on board. It's crucial that the people living in your house and using the space on a daily basis—whoever they are—know how important it is (and how important it is to *you*) to keep up your hard work.

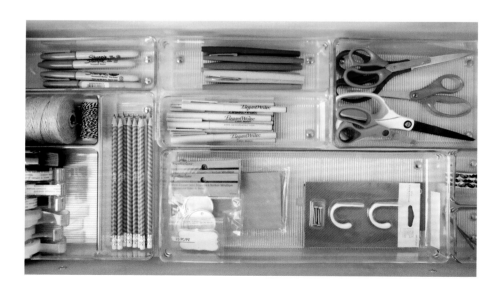

ONE IN, ONE OUT

This is not always a popular rule, but it helps to avoid the ultimate catastrophe of undoing everything you've worked toward. It comes into play after you've whipped your space into shape . . . and then you start accumulating more things. The good news is that a well-conceived system not only accommodates what you already own but also has enough flexibility built in for future items.

But a good system will only get you so far if you start going overboard with buying sweaters or hoarding extra tubes of toothpaste. We like to think of it as being similar to the 80/20 rule of not overeating—you don't want to eat until you're 100 percent full, or so full that all you can do after a meal is lie on the couch. Ideally you'd eat only until you were 80 percent full—satisfied, but still comfortable. The same goes for organizing: You want to leave a little room so that if you buy new things like a new pair of shoes, another jacket, or a pack of toilet paper that was on sale, you'll still be able to fit it comfortably in the space and have that nice, airy feel. If you start abusing that extra space and shoving things into every nook and cranny, you'll lose that lovely uncluttered vibe that makes a space feel neat and accessible.

A space that's completely crammed with stuff is like the storage equivalent of loosening your belt after too many french fries. Even though you can make room, it doesn't feel good, and it also compromises the integrity of the organizational system (and your self-esteem). That's why we recommend making sure that if you're bringing things in, you're also taking things out. As we always say: You can have the item or you can have the space, but you can't have *both*. We're not going to stand next to your bathroom vanity with a baseball bat trying to intimidate you from shoving in that extra moisturizer you *had* to have—it's your home, you can do what you want—but hopefully we can make you feel just the right amount of accountable to make good choices that ensure the well-being and longevity of your newly organized space. But if picturing us holding a baseball bat is more effective motivation for you, then go for it. It's your organizational journey, and we are just here to support the ride!

HOW *to* STAY INSPIRED

If you ever start to feel the clutter creeping back into your life (it can do that), escape to these sites, Instagrams, and stores to feel reenergized and motivated to refresh your space. Sometimes a few new magazine holders or a pretty box for your bookshelf is enough to keep your room in check.

SITES *to* STALK

GOOP
goop.com

LAUREN CONRAD
laurenconrad.com

A CUP OF JO
cupofjo.com

MARTHA STEWART
marthastewart.com

YOUNG HOUSE LOVE
younghouselove.com

OH JOY!
ohjoy.com

A BEAUTIFUL MESS
abeautifulmess.com

HELLO SUNSHINE
hello-sunshine.com

TIFFANI THIESSEN
tiffanithiessen.com

JENNI KAYNE / RIP & TAN
jennikayne.com

DOMINO
domino.com

STYLE ME PRETTY
stylemepretty.com/living

INSTAGRAMS *to* FOLLOW

@GOOP

@JOANNAGAINES

@MARIEKONDO

@DARCYMILLER

@LOVEANDLION

@ELSIELARSON

@ABEAUTIFULMESS

@INSPIRE_ME_HOME_DECOR

@BPATRICKFLYNN

@MRORLANDOSORIA

@MOLLYBSIMS

@PENCILANDPAPERCO

@ALYSSAROSENHECK

@LAURENCONRAD

@VALLEYBRINKROAD

@REESESBOOKCLUBXHELLOSUNSHINE

STORES *to* SHOP

ARAM
aram.co.uk

ARGOS
argos.co.uk

DUNELM
dunelm.com

GREAT LITTLE TRADING CO.
gltc.co.uk

H&M
hm.com

HABITAT
habitat.co.uk

HEAL'S
heals.com

HOBBYCRAFT
hobbycraft.co.uk

IKEA
ikea.com

JOHN LEWIS
johnlewis.com

LAKELAND
lakeland.co.uk

M&S
marksandspencer.com

MADE
made.com

MUJI
muji.com

NEXT
next.co.uk

OLIVER BONAS
oliverbonas.com

SCP
scp.co.uk

STORE
aplaceforeverything.co.uk

THE CONRAN SHOP
conranshop.co.uk

THE HOLDING COMPANY
theholdingcompany.co.uk

THE RANGE
therange.co.uk

WEST ELM
westelm.com

thanks

Thank you to my husband, John, and my kids, Stella Blue and Sutton Gray. I know you thought this day would never come, Stella, but the book really IS done this time. And a huge thank-you to Jamie for holding my family *and* business together, to my parents for being my biggest supporters, to my mother, Roberta, for being my greatest influence, to my mother-in-law, Liz, for always being there, and to my brother, Dashiell, who is the *real* writer in the family—I love you all more than words could ever say.

—*Clea*

To my grandfather A. Aaron Elkind, who always dreamed big and taught us all to do the same, to my grandmother Rosella who has unequivocally championed every single one of my businesses, to my parents Sari and Stuart, sister Alexis, aunt Marcy, in-laws Gail and Marvin, grandparents Rita and Erv, and last but definitely not least my husband Jeremy and children Miles and Marlowe for ENDLESSLY supporting this wild ride.

—*Joanna*

We could not have ever (EVER) completed this book without the support and contributions from our INCREDIBLE team, agent Lindsay Edgecombe, editor Angelin Borsics, designer Mia Johnson, production manager Kim Tyner, production editor Abby Oladipo, compositor Alexandria Martinez, and managing editor Aislinn Belton. Lastly, a very special thanks to all of our fans, followers, and clients.

INDEX

American Girl mania, 150
appliances, kitchen, 69, 227, 231
arts-and-crafts closet, 137
art studio, 129
art supplies, 134, 137, 158

baby bottles, 205, 206
backpacks, 56, 58, 172
ballroom closet, 178–80
bare-bones closet, 176
baskets, lined, 45
baskets with handles, 45
bathrooms, 90–115
    arranging by scent, 113
    back stock cabinet, 114
    countertop storage, 109
    daily drawer, 98
    guest bathroom drawer, 106
    linen closet open shelving, 102
    with no drawers, 97
    pretty stockpile shelf, 105
    under sink storage, 100–101
    skin saving cabinet, 93
    skin saving drawer, 94
    storage closet in, 110
batteries, 193
beach supplies, 62
beads, 118, 157
beverages, 219, 224
bill-paying setup, 130
bins, clear, 45, 87, 105
bins, lined, 45
blenders, 227
books, 122, 145, 158
boots, 171, 175, 183
breakfast items, 217, 219, 223, 227, 228, 235, 236, 239, 240
business documents, 130

cabinet pantry, 216–17
cabinets
    back stock, 83, 114

for bathroom supplies, 110
but-wait-there's-more, 114
glass-front, 209
for laundry essentials, 72
medicine cabinets, 93
skin saving, 93
supply cabinet, 134
caddies, 105, 134, 198
canisters, 209, 223, 228
cards and notecards, 125, 130, 133
carts, freestanding, 97, 176
chalk, sidewalk, 147
chargers, 94
charms, 118
chef's pantry, 220
Christina Applegate's mudroom, 69
cleaning supplies, 76, 84, 110, 198
closets, 164–89
    for adult hobbies, 186
    arts-and-crafts, 137
    ballroom, 178–80
    bare-bones, 176
    in bathroom, 110
    cleaning, rules for, 165
    coat closet, 66
    craft, 153
    Kacey Musgraves's, 188
    for men, 185
    multipurpose, 65
    with no dresser, 168
    Rachel Zoe's, 167
    school and sports, 172
    for shoes, 171
    small space, 183
    Thomas Rhett Akins's, 175
    for toys, 148
clothing, getting rid of, 165
coat closet, 66
coffee station, 197
color, sorting by, 47
cotton swabs, 94
craft closet, 153

craft supplies, 125, 157, 161
crayons, 142, 161
cutlery, 194, 201

desk space, 89
desktops, 126, 154
detergents, 72, 75, 76, 80, 86
diapers, 83, 161
docking station, 122
document boxes, 122, 130
dolls, 150, 158
door racks, 44, 84
drawers
    craft cup, 157
    for daily bathroom items, 98
    drawer inserts for, 94
    "go play outside," 147
    guest bathroom, 106
    junk-no-more, 193
    kids' dishes, 205
    "Mom, I need a pencil!," 121
    nursing supplies, 206
    for pantry, 232, 235
    paper-lined, 194
    school supplies, 142
    skin saving, 94
    starting organization with, 27
dressers, makeshift, 168

editing process, 25
    create groupings, 34
    getting rid of things, 36–41
    pantry, 215
    taking everything out, 33
electronics, 122
Elfa door organizers, 153
Elfa wall unit, 154
entertaining supplies, 66, 86, 194, 201, 209
entryways, 54–69
    beachy mudroom, 62
    Christina Applegate's mudroom, 69

coat closet, 66
makeshift, 56
Molly Sim's mudroom, 61
multipurpose closet, 65
traditional mudroom, 58
essentials cabinet, 72

facial products, 93, 98, 105, 113
file folders, 130
first-aid supplies, 65, 69, 110
flashlights, 193
fragrances, 113
fridge, glass-front, 210
fridge and freezer storage, 202

games and puzzles, 158
getting rid of things
closet items, 165
kids' play items, 141
rationalizing, 36–37
rules for, 41
tips for, 37–38
gift supplies, 75, 89, 121, 133,
137, 162
glass-front cabinets, 209
glass-front fridge, 210
guest bathroom drawer, 106
Gwyneth Paltrow's playroom,
158

hair care products, 100–101,
105
hampers, 79, 89
handbags, 183, 188
hangers, 44, 66, 167
hanging wall unit, 161
hats, 62, 175, 176, 185
home office, 116–37
arts-and-crafts closet, 137
art studio, 129
command station, 130
jewelry studio, 118
Joy Cho's, 125
Lauren Conrad's crafting
closet, 133
"Mom, I need a pencil!"
drawer, 121
office on a wall, 126
smokey storage shelves, 122
supply cabinet, 134

homework flashcards, 148
homework folders, 145
homework station, 154
hooks, 56, 58, 61, 69, 176, 183,
186
household paperwork, 130
household supplies, 76, 79,
83, 86

jackets, 167, 175, 178, 186
jewelry, 180, 188
jewelry studio, 118
Joy Cho's home office, 125
junk-no-more drawer, 193

Kacey Musgraves's closet, 188
Karen Fairchild's laundry room,
89
kitchens, 190–211
coffee station, 197
entertaining cabinet, 201
fridge and freezer, 202
glass-front cabinets, 209
glass-front fridge, 210
junk-no-more drawer,
193
kids' dishes drawer, 205
nursing drawer, 206
paper-lined drawer, 194
under skin storage, 198
knitting supplies, 137
Kondo, Marie, 168

labels, 49–51
laundry rooms, 70–89
back stock cabinets, 83
don't-forget-the-door
solution, 84
dos and don'ts, 80
endless loads of laundry
cabinet, 80
essentials cabinet, 72
giant utility room, 79
Karen Fairchild's, 89
with no storage, 75
open shelf solution, 86
with single shelf, 76
Lauren Conrad's crafting
closet, 133
lazy Susan, 44

LEGOs, 145, 148, 158
linen closet open shelving,
102
linens, 176, 201
low-bar lifestyle, 26–27

magazine files, 44, 145, 153
mail and packages, 69
mailing supplies, 125
makeshift entry, 56
makeup products, 101, 109
Mandy Moore's pantry, 231
medications, adult, 65
medicine cabinets, 93
Molly Sim's mudroom, 61
mudrooms
beachy, 62
Christina Applegate's, 69
Molly Sim's, 61
traditional, 58
multipurpose closet, 65

nail polish, 105, 114
napkin rings, 201
no-storage laundry room, 75
nursing supplies, 206

open shelving, 86
organization. See also editing
process
benefits of, 20–21
easy projects, 29
editing process, 25
embracing low-bar lifestyle,
26–27
form and function, 46
guidance and help for, 22
hard projects, 31
labeling items, 49–51
medium projects, 29
mindset for, 19
sorting by color, 47
tips for long-term success,
243–45
outdoor supplies, 76, 201

paint bottles, 129
paintbrushes, 129, 134
paint supplies, 137, 147,
153

pantry, 212–41
    black-and-white, 227
    build-your-own, 224
    chef's pantry, 220
    editing process, 215
    food storage cabinet, 216–17
    food storage rules, 219
    freestanding food storage, 219
    Gwyneth Paltrow's, 240
    Mandy Moore's, 231
    for morning routine, 223
    no-pantry solution, 232
    no-pantry solution, part two, 235
    Park Avenue, 228
    for snack items, 236
    wire shelving, 239
paper-lined drawer, 194
paper towels, 231
Park Avenue pantry, 228
party supplies, 137, 162
peg board, 126, 154
pens and pencils, 121, 142, 153, 154, 162
personal-care items, 83
pharmacy items, 69, 110
photo boxes, 125, 133
placemats, 201
play spaces, 138–63
    American Girl obsessed, 150
    craft cup drawer, 157
    deep craft closet, 153
    easy-access toy closet, 148
    getting rid of stuff, 141
    "go play outside" drawer, 147
    Gwyneth Paltrow's playroom, 158
    hanging toy shelves, 161
    posh playroom, 145
    school supply drawer, 142
    study station, 154
    under-stair storage, 162
printer paper, 122, 134
puzzles, 158

Rachel Zoe's closet, 167
rainbow sorting order, 47
ROYGBIV (sorting by color), 47
running shoes, 175, 176

sandals, 171, 176, 183, 185
scent-based categories, 113, 114
school paperwork, 130, 145
school supplies, 134, 142
school uniforms, 172
science kits, 158
seasonal items, 58, 65, 175, 178, 188
sewing supplies, 162
shelf liner, 239
shelves
    hanging toy shelves, 161
    linen closet open shelving, 102
    open shelving, 86
    pretty stockpile shelf, 105
    single, for laundry room, 76
    smokey storage shelves, 122
    tiered, 45
    under-shelf organizers, 110
    wire shelving pantry, 239
shirts, 168, 175, 178
shoe boxes, 44, 183
shoes, 62, 65, 69, 171, 172, 175, 176, 180, 183, 185, 188
sidewalk chalk, 147
sinks, storage under, 100–101, 198
skin saving cabinet, 93
skin saving drawer, 94
small space closet, 183
snacks, 224, 228, 232, 235, 236, 239, 240
sneakers, 183
soaps, 198
socks, 168
spice jars, 231, 232
sponges, 72, 84, 198
sports items, 61
sports uniforms, 69, 86, 172
spray bottles, 110
stackable storage, 76
stairs, storage under, 162
stand mixer, 224
staplers, 121
stationery, 133
storage inserts, 44
storage items
    essential items, 44–45
    shopping for, 42–43

storage tiers, 45
study station, 154
supply cabinet, 134
swimsuits, 172, 186

tables, for entryway, 56
tape dispensers, 121
tea accessories, 197
tea boxes, 223
tea supplies, 232
Thomas Rhett Akins's closet, 175
toilet paper, 83, 97, 102, 110
tools, 79, 193
toothbrushes, 98
toothpaste, 98, 106
tote bags, 186
towels, 61, 62, 97, 102, 126
toy closet, 148
train sets, 148
travel items, 122, 176
turntables, 110, 145, 217

utensils, 194, 205
utensil trays, 194

vegetables, storing, 202

wall space, for office items, 126
wall units, 97
water bottles, 69, 219, 231
wire shelving pantry, 239
workbooks, 145
workout clothes, 180

yarn, 133

An Hachette UK Company
www.hachette.co.uk

Published in Great Britain in 2019 by Mitchell Beazley,
an imprint of Octopus Publishing Group Ltd
Carmelite House
50 Victoria Embankment
London EC4Y 0DZ
www.octopusbooks.co.uk

ISBN 978-1-784-72594-5

A CIP catalogue record for this book is available from the British Library.

Printed in China

Cover and interior design by Mia Johnson
Photography and illustrations by The Home Edit

10 9 8 7 6 5 4 3 2

bakery	cheese
condiments	dairy
fruit	kids'
meals	produce
protein	snacks
sweets	veggies

cheese

bakery

dairy

condiments

kids'

fruit

produce

meats

snacks

protein

veggies

sweets